REVIEWS BY LEADERS

'I wish they'd given me this book along with our $49M Series C round of funding. It would have been equally valuable. Essential wisdom put into a clear structure that is memorable and actionable.'

Darrell Benatar, President and Executive Chairman, UserTesting, Inc

'This book is mandatory reading for anyone who cares about becoming a leader. As Mr. Wyatt aptly points out, leaders aren't born they are made; and his remarkable book will help you hone your skills to unlock your leadership potential. Bring a pen and prepare yourself - this isn't just a book it's a graduate level course on how to think, decide, act and lead - a must read for all aspiring leaders!'

Alden Mills, author of *Unstoppable Teams: The Four Essential Actions of High-Performance Leadership,* (Harper Business, 2019) and *Be Unstoppable*, (Tilbury House Publishers, 2019), Inc 500 CEO and former Navy SEAL platoon commander.

'Unlike most business books that can be summarized in a page or two, Wyatt provides practical, no-nonsense advice on five

different modes of leadership. Whether you're a senior leader looking to refresh your skills or a new manager developing your leadership toolkit, this book is for you.'

Chris Hicken, General Partner, HFF Capital

'At several stages in my professional life I have worked with and for Stuart Wyatt. And he has also worked for me. That has enabled me to witness that by employing the five modes of leadership people can strike an effective balance between motivational positivism and down to earth coordination of people and resources. I have seen the results, up close and personal. It works.'

Steve C. Brazier, CEO of HexCel Designs,
ex Director of Global Education at Promethean.
Discoverer of the mathematical principle upon
which the Arokah puzzle is based.

'The Five Modes of Leadership delivers a compelling playbook for getting the best out of your team and yourself. The ideas are presented in a style that is easy to read, easy to remember, and easy to implement.'

Brent Lang, Chairman & CEO
Vocera Communications, Inc.

'An indispensable reference book for anyone serious about management and leadership.'

Joe Cussens, Managing Director,
The Bath Pub Company Ltd

'Stuart Wyatt is the most disciplined and effective business leader I've met. This book represents the practices I've personally seen him employ successfully over the past 30 years. Every leader and manager should read this book and consider using its lessons to achieve heightened success.'

Mike Faith, CEO, Headsets.com, Inc.

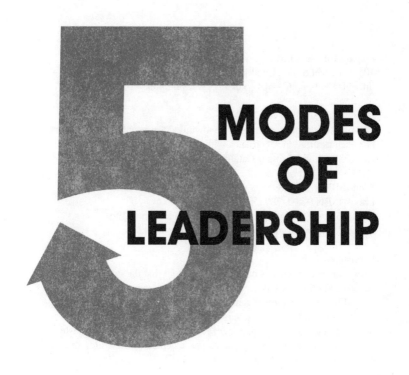

5 MODES OF LEADERSHIP

STUART WYATT

Legend Business Ltd,
107-111 Fleet Street, London, EC4A 2AB
info@legend-paperbooks.co.uk I www.legendpress.co.uk

Contents © Stuart Wyatt 2019
The right of the above author to be identified as the author of this work
has been asserted in accordance with the Copyright, Designs and Patents
Act 1988. British Library Cataloguing in Publication Data available.

Print ISBN 978-1-7895507-7-1
Ebook ISBN 978-1-7895507-8-8
Set in Times. Printing managed by Jellyfish Solutions Ltd
Cover design by Tom Sanderson I www.the-parish.com

Publishers Note
Every possible effort has been made to ensure that the information
contained in this book is accurate at the time of going to press, and
the publishers and authors cannot accept responsibility for any errors
or omissions, however caused. No responsibility for loss or damage
occasioned to any person acting, or refraining from action, as a result
of the material in this publication can be accepted by the editor, the
publisher or any of the authors.

Thank you Liza Paderes and Tom Chalmers of Legend Business for believing in this book. I am also extremely grateful to the many managers and leaders who have given me helpful feedback. There are too many to name, though I must especially thank Ania Wyatt and David Carey, who gave me very thorough and valuable critiques. Barry Faith also played a pivotal role by providing long-term encouragement and support. And thank you to my agent Robin Wade and my wife Terri, who guides my writing towards becoming comprehensible. Without those two, this book would probably not exist.

The Five Modes of Leadership

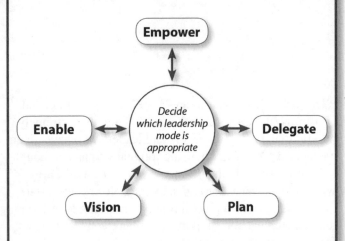

You adopt the appropriate mode of leadership for the situation. As you lead your team you will switch back and forth between modes, matching your approach to the circumstances. And you may often select different modes for leading different people.

INTRODUCTION

Dear Reader,

Great leaders adopt different modes of action at different times. For example, sometimes the leader is unwavering in his or her resolve to see a commitment through to the end. And yet, on another occasion, that same leader appears to instinctively know when to drop some scheme as hopeless and set off in a new direction. And then there is handling people...

Sometimes, we see the leader intently listening as he or she consults team members, employing an inclusive consultative style. But then, on another occasion, the leader domineeringly hands out orders and expects obedient, instant action.

We may see the leader metaphorically roll up his or her sleeves and lead from the front, but at other times he or she disappears for a while and then later re-emerges to share a new vision of success. The most effective leaders appear to effortlessly switch between different styles of leadership. They seem to instinctively know what to do and when to do it.

What appears at first to be instinct is more likely to be the result of study, training and practice. We can divide their actions into five very different modes of leadership: *Vision, Plan, Delegate, Enable*, and *Empower*. This book explains those Five Modes of Leadership, when to adopt each mode and what actions to take. And you will read many more insights into effective leadership with plenty of 'how to' guidance.

Considering your own experience, have you been on the receiving end of poor leadership? You probably have because the prevailing quality of leadership is very poor. That is good news for you because it means you can stand out from the crowd and enjoy uncommon success. This book will show you how to lead people so that they willingly work for you, with their efforts coordinated effectively and their minds focussed upon producing the outcomes you want.

The Five Modes of Leadership gives you a simple, but not simplistic, way to navigate through the complexities of leading people. But first, we must dispel one big falsehood.

The idea that a few people are born leaders and the rest of us suffer some great disadvantage is just not true. For example, people often use Napoleon Bonaparte (1769–1821) as an example to support the born leader argument. It is true that as a child, Napoleon Bonaparte's classmates nicknamed him 'Little Corporal' because he always wanted to be the person in charge. His desire to lead was there, but he did not yet have the ability. Napoleon enrolled at a leading military academy where he studied the great military leaders of the past. He then honed his leadership skills as a junior artillery officer.

Napoleon's efforts paid off with a breakthrough at only 26 years of age. He was promoted to commander of France's largest army, the Army of the Interior. As you probably know, Napoleon later rose to become Emperor of the French and King of Italy. He was a determined man with a desire to lead people, the motivation to learn and a willingness to accept responsibility and practise his skills.

The fact you have chosen to read this book suggests that you already share the first two of Napoleon's traits, the desire to lead and the motivation to learn. If you read this book and put the ideas into action you will also be employing Napoleon's other traits: taking responsibility, action and practice. Leadership does not entail some magic ingredient but a set of basic methods and skills that anyone of average intelligence can learn.

There are many oversized books about management and leadership. You may therefore be wondering if it is possible to condense the most important lessons of leadership into a compact book like this. The answer most certainly is *YES*!

I imagine you to be a busy person with little time available for reading and study. I have therefore attempted to keep the text short, to the point, easy to assimilate and always focussed upon effective action.

During thirty plus years of experience as a manager, trainer, interim executive and management consultant I have found that when one divides the potential leadership actions into five distinct modes of action one can more easily see through the clutter and complexities. These are the Five Modes of Leadership. I, and others, have taught the lessons in this book to managers and leaders at all levels and in a variety of organisations. The result has been that people who employed the Five Modes of Leadership reported that they quickly become more effective and received respect for their leadership skills.

I offer no magic-wand solutions. At times, it may not be easy. As Theodore Roosevelt[1] said, *'Nothing great was ever achieved without effort.'* But stick at it and the rewards will surely come.

The Five Modes of Leadership show you how to proactively analyse your situation and decide on the most appropriate actions. This will enable you to experience greater control over events and people, which increases the general level of confidence of your team and inspires people to follow your lead. By acting in the appropriate leadership mode, you will bring people along with you to share your vision of success. They will willingly work to achieve your goal. And you will enable them to perform to the best of their abilities, which in turn serves to stoke the fire of their motivation.

---

1. Statesman, author, explorer, soldier, naturalist and reformer. 26th President of the United States of America.

A reminder. Reading is good, but only our actions make a difference. As you read, I urge you to learn, to think, to decide, and to **act** — repeatedly. You will surely reap significant rewards from your efforts.

Best wishes for the journey ahead.
Stuart Wyatt

'Leadership is the art of getting someone else to do something you want done because he [or she] wants to do it.'

Dwight D. Eisenhower, 1890–1969,
34th President of the United States of America,
Supreme Commander of the Allied Forces in Europe
during World War II

CONTENTS

'If your actions inspire others to dream more, learn more, do more and become more, you are a leader.'

John Quincy Adams, 1767–1848,
6th President of the United States of America

DEFINITIONS

Leadership:
Establishing a clear vision and sharing that vision with others
so they willingly follow. Providing the information, knowledge
and methods to realize that vision. Inspiring people to perform
and engage in achieving a goal. The activity of leading a group
of people or the ability to do this.

Mode:
A possible, customary, or preferred way of doing something.
A way of behaving, especially one that becomes instinctive,
familiar, or habitual.

Vision:
The ability to think about or plan the future with imagination or
wisdom. A vivid image of what the future will or could be like.

Goal:
A desired end outcome.

Objective:
One of many definable steps or measures of progress needed
to achieve the goal referred to above.

Project:
An individual or collaborative enterprise to achieve a goal, often constrained by objectives for time, quality and cost, which are commonly referred to as the triple constraints

---

'A leader is a dealer in hope.'
Napoléon Bonaparte, 1769–1821,
Emperor of the French and King of Italy

HOW TO GET THE BEST FROM THIS BOOK

1. Read Part One, which explains how belief, systematic organisation, leadership and management all fit together to create the setting in which to use the Five Modes of Leadership.
2. Read Part Two, where you consider both your personal and your team's perceptions.
3. You could read Part Three straight through, but you will gain much more at this point and in the future if you:
    a) Consider a goal you are now working upon.
    b) Use the perceptions diagrams in chapters 9 and 11 to select the appropriate mode of leadership to adopt: Vision, Plan, Delegate, Enable or Empower.
    c) Read the chapter explaining the mode you will adopt and the suggested leadership actions. Take action and achieve the objectives.
    d) Repeat the above steps a), b) & c) above as you incorporate all five modes into your leadership skill-set.

- Read the 'How to' Guides in Part Four as necessary when indicated in chapters.
- Part Five provides quick reference copies of the diagrams and checklists in the book.

Suggested Reading Order

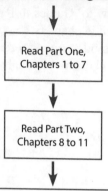

Read Part One,
Chapters 1 to 7

Read Part Two,
Chapters 8 to 11

Refer to Part Three as you start to employ the modes of leadership on a 'real' current goal

a) Consider a goal you are now working upon.

b) Use the perceptions diagrams in chapters 9 and 11 to select the appropriate mode of leadership to adopt: Vision, Plan, Delegate, Enable or Empower.

c) Read the chapter explaining the mode you will adopt and the suggested leadership actions. Take action and achieve the objectives.

Repeat the above steps a) to c) as you incorporate all five modes into your leadership skill-set.

Read How To Guides in Part 4 as necessary.

Refer to Quick Reference in Part 5 as necessary.

KEY POINTS SO FAR

- It is a myth that leaders are born. With application, anyone of basic intelligence and above can be a very effective leader.
- Leadership requires positive, proactive action. The leadership sequence is: learn, think, decide, act.
- With application, almost anyone can become an exceptionally good leader. And the transformation from average to outstanding can be astonishingly fast.

'Excellence is an art won by training and habituation. We do not act rightly because we have virtue or excellence, but we rather have those because we have acted rightly. We are what we repeatedly do. Excellence, then, is not an act but a habit.'
Aristotle, 384 BC–322 BC
Ancient Greek Philosopher, Scientist & Physician.

'Whatever you are, be a good one.'

Abraham Lincoln, 1809–1865
16th President of the United States of America,
led the United States through its Civil War,
abolished slavery and modernised the economy.

PART ONE

HOW BELIEF, SYSTEMATIC ORGANISATION, LEADERSHIP AND MANAGEMENT ALL FIT TOGETHER

CHAPTER 1

PERCEPTION IS THE GATEKEEPER TO RESULTS

Some people arrive at work each day to robotically spend their day. That may be perfectly acceptable in some types of job. For example, on some factory production lines or in shipping departments the worker repeats a sequence of simple tasks so many times they hardly need to think about their work. This diminishes as computer controlled automation takes over and makes that type of work redundant.

In the future, we can expect many more roles to convert from requiring human effort to being automated and controlled by computer. So, it is almost certain that your people must use their minds at least as much as their brawn. Their freethinking complicates matters for you, the leader.

As they think about you, their work and their teammates, they continuously form perceptions about the work ahead. One of the things they consider, consciously or subconsciously, is the likelihood of forthcoming success or failure. And, of course, you do the same. Let us assess these thoughts and rate your chances for success.

CONSIDER YOUR CURRENT GOALS AT WORK

First, write a list that names each of your current goals[2]. Do that now…

For each item on your list, now rate your team's likelihood of success. For each goal, choose the most appropriate answer from the list of nine alternatives below. Write the answer against each item as a number from 1 to 9.

For example, if one goal was to 'Move office' and you felt certain you would achieve this perfectly by the required date, you would rate that goal '9' and enter the score '9' on your list next to the goal.

Here are the nine alternative answers.

1. I wish I could answer but I am not even sure what my team should achieve.
2. I am not certain how to answer because there is no way that I can know what the likelihood of success really is. We will just have to do our best and see how things pan out.
3. I am confident in the ability of my team and myself, but I know enough about my job to say that some of our current goals are unrealistic and unattainable.
4. I really would like to feel more confident, but the reality is that I am not sure it is possible to achieve our goals.
5. It is possible but it is going to be a struggle.
6. We should succeed in some areas but may well miss other goals.
7. We have an even-odds likelihood of success.
8. There is a very good chance, but it is not a foregone conclusion.

2. The terms 'goal' and 'objective' have a similar meaning in common language. However, in this book (and in project management), goals and objectives mean different things. Goals refer to the desired end outcome from a chunk of work, the final goal. And each objective is one of possibly many definable measures of progress, or steps, needing to be achieved on the way to achieving the end goal, the desired end result. See also definitions on page 16.

9. I am certain we will achieve our goals on time, to the desired quality, with the available resources (on time, on quality, on budget).

Rate your goals now…

Now you have a list of goals, each with a 1 to 9 score. The higher the score the better. Next, switch viewpoint and look from the perspective of your team members. Endeavour to see the work ahead as they would.

CONSIDER TEAM MEMBERS' PERCEPTIONS

Consider each of your key people, one at a time. In your mind, set them free to speak from the heart and tell you straight. Theoretically at this point, which of the nine previous options would each person select to describe your team's likelihood of forthcoming success?

This exercise is well worth the time and thought. List your key people and note down the answer you would expect from each person…

It matters very much how each of your team members would answer. Their views offer an important guide to whether you and your team are heading towards forthcoming success or failure. That is because your team's belief in success or failure has a direct and substantial effect upon their effort, their performance and therefore your results.

If your people do not believe they can do something, they will either deliver a sub-standard performance or more likely fail altogether. Likewise, if you do not think you can do something, you will probably fail. This is because *perception is the gatekeeper to results*.

When you give people a new job to complete, or a deadline to meet, they at once start thinking ahead. They assess how the work will mesh with their existing workload. They ponder their ability to do the work. We all do this, but in varying degrees of detail and with varying levels of ability to accurately assess the situation.

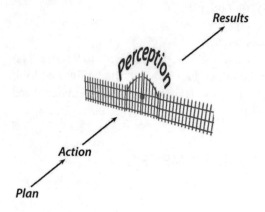

- Do we possess the necessary skills and resources?
- Will we find the work easy or tough?
- What hurdles will be in our way?
- Will we need to rely upon other people?
- Might they let us down?
- Is it possible we shall fail?

We temper any natural enthusiasm (or pessimism) as we consider the reality of the challenge ahead. We ponder any obvious risks and speculate upon the potential for unforeseen problems to arise. Then, having weighed up those factors, we form a judgment about the probability of success or failure.

Many people do not follow the above thought processes as systematically. Many will jump to an immediate decision based upon gut feeling. Whichever way we go about it, we soon form an opinion that falls somewhere between the two extremes of *'We can easily do this'* and *'This is impossible.'*

Whichever way people think, be it considered, reasoned or intuitive, informed or uninformed, prejudiced or open-minded, off-the-wall or wise, everyone in your team has an opinion. Be assured, their perceptions significantly affect your chances of success as a leader.

THE INFLUENCE OF BELIEF UPON SUCCESS

The arena in which people's belief in success or failure is most openly displayed is professional sport. For example, listen to the interview of a winning Olympic athlete. He or she often reveals how belief played an essential part in their success.[3]

For example, after winning Wimbledon for a record eighth time in 2017, the tennis player Roger Federer said that, *'It's just belief you know...if you believe you can go really far in your life. I believed, and I did it.'*

On the other hand, when the interviewer moves on to speak with the loser, you will often detect language that betrays a lack of belief. They say something like, *'I did my best but I knew it was going to be difficult,'* or even *'I'm not yet ready for this level of competition.'*

At work, the power of belief is not so openly on display but the impact is just the same. You will have experienced how your own belief has influenced your results for good or ill. Of course, it is the same for everyone in your team.

Federico Fellini, the Italian film producer, was familiar with leading large and expensive projects. He said, *'Our minds shape the way a thing will be, because we act according to our expectations.'* Henry Ford, the founder of Ford Motor Company in 1901, put it this way, *'Whether you think you can or cannot, you are probably right.'* Perceptions exert a powerful controlling influence over your people's quality of effort, levels of energy, degree of creative thinking and more.

Thus, many leaders who understand the importance of a positive attitude will insist the solution is for everyone to talk only of success. Positive affirmations become part of the team's everyday language: *'We have a can-do attitude. There is no such thing as problems. We overcome all challenges.*

---

3. There have been many academic studies on this subject, for example: *Self-Talk in Sport and Performance*, Judy L. Van Raalte (Professor of Psychology, Springfield College) and Andrew Vincent (Oxford University Press, 2017).

We are the best.' And so on. Expressing these positives does lift the mood. But is this reality? Can belief alone achieve all? Surely, some things must genuinely be impossible, or is positivity all powerful?

The rise of positive thinking in western society owes much to one minister in the Reformed Church of America. He moved to Manhattan, New York, in 1932. Next door to his new church was a psychiatric outpatient clinic. The minister and his psychoanalyst neighbour became friends. They worked together helping people who had mentally hit rock-bottom as they tried to cope with life. The minister, Norman Vincent Peale, observed how adopting a continually positive approach would enable people to turn around their physical and mental health, help them out of the abyss, and often improve their fortunes.

After 20 years of experience he wrote a seminal book: *The Power of Positive Thinking*.[4] That book spawned an entire self-help industry that continues today, with millions of books sold each year and thousands of so-called self-help gurus selling their services. Peale's book came before sixty years of serious psychological research and recent scientific investigation of the human brain.

Magnetic Resonance Imaging (MRI) scanners enable scientists to picture brain activity as a person responds to repeated positive thought patterns. Over time, these repeated patterns alter the pathways and physical construction of the brain.[5] We now understand much more about how our minds respond to positive thoughts and thereby influence our actions and so our outcomes. And, interestingly, the result of all that scientific study confirms what Peale wrote back in 1952. It works like this…

When we repeatedly direct our feelings, words, vision, emotions and actions we create physical changes in our brains.

---

4. *The Power of Positive Thinking*, by Dr. Norman Vincent Peale (1898–1993), continuously in print since first published in 1952.

5. For a summary of authoritative academic articles read *Constructive and Unconstructive Repetitive Thought* (published 2008 by the American Psychological Association, by Prof. Edward R. Watkins, University of Exeter).

We must act upon several fronts. First, we identify which of our current beliefs align with our goals. Those beliefs form the foundations upon which we construct our desired new beliefs.

Secondly, we proactively direct our thoughts to see in our mind's eye the achievement of our goals. We involve our self-talk and our emotions. Some people say they experience an internal movie with positive dialogue, live action, vivid colour and emotional power. They see, hear, feel and even smell their imagined forthcoming success. They repeat this visualisation many times until they firmly believe they will achieve their goals.

Inevitably, our beliefs exert a very strong influence over how we act, and how much mental and physical effort we devote to achieving our goals. Thus, our thoughts affect our actions and in turn our probability of success. If we surround ourselves with a team of like-minded people, each person's confidence multiplies as the common belief grows that *'We can do this.'*

CONFIRMATION BIAS

At this point, it pays to be aware of a bias that can creep into our thinking and inflate our belief beyond reality. We can be influenced by an effect called *confirmation bias*.

We humans are fascinatingly complex. We have extraordinary abilities to reason and to process information. But our minds also contain various glitches that can trip us up. One of these is the human tendency toward confirmation bias. As Warren Buffett[6] put it, *'What the human being is best at doing is interpreting all new information so that prior conclusions remain intact.'*

There are two consequences of confirmation bias that you need to watch out for. The first is this — when we truly believe

---

6. Born in Nebraska, USA in 1930, and often called the Oracle of Omaha, Warren Buffett is one of the richest and most respected businessmen and philanthropists in the world.

something is happening, or going to happen, we tend to interpret new facts and observations as confirming our belief. Thus, we may see a certain fact as proof that we are progressing towards our goal, whilst another person might look at the very same fact and consider it indicates the opposite, that we are less likely to achieve our goal. If we fall under the influence of confirmation bias we will totally ignore the other person's point of view, even branding them as foolish.

For example, you will surely have observed the following. A right-wing person will typically read right-wing news sources and decry the left-wing newspapers as printing lies and rubbish. Meanwhile, his or her left-wing friend will do the exact opposite and both people remain convinced they are the only ones who take the factual, knowledgeable stance.

People often feed their minds with information that supports their already embedded point of view, which serves to further strengthen their existing beliefs and thereby exclude other, potentially valid, points of view.[7]

Even scientists, who take pride in their objectivity, are frequently caught out, which is one of the reasons why the scientific community relies upon multiple peer reviews as a test of validity for any new ideas.

Another example: we occasionally see executives latch on to the significance of one report that supports a previous decision whilst criticising a different report that contains information which contradicts the wisdom of their decision. Whilst doing this, the executive remains unaware that he or she has succumbed to confirmation bias.

CONCLUSIONS

All the above means that as you foster your own and your team's belief in forthcoming success you must be careful to

---

7. For a more detail introduction, consider reading the paper *Confirmation Bias: A Ubiquitous Phenomenon in Many Guises,* by Raymond S. Nickerson, Tufts University (Copyright 1998 by the Educational Publishing Foundation).

remain rooted in reality. We need to be positive and remain realistic at the same time. That means we may need to consider opposing ideas at the same time.

One way to do this is to follow the example of the scientific community and occasionally subject your work to external review. Find one or more people outside your team who can deliver a dispassionate and cold opinion of your plans and progress. They will either validate your opinion or help you become aware of blind spots that may have slipped under your radar due to confirmation bias.

Yes, positive thinking works, and is very important. Many leaders focus all their energies upon building a positive vision of success. However, do not think this book is leading you towards relying upon the power of positive thinking. That would be over simplistic. And you will not be encouraged to pump up your team's beliefs to an artificial high. No — our journey leads along a more down-to-earth path. At this point, just note the crucial truth that *perception is the gatekeeper to results*.

'All our knowledge has its origins in our perceptions.'
Leonardo da Vinci, 1452–1519,
Italian polymath, painter, sculptor, architect,
musician, mathematician, engineer, inventor,
anatomist, geologist, cartographer, botanist, and writer.

CHAPTER 2

GOALS AND PROJECTS

In 1903, a forty-two-year-old engineer was writing a ground-breaking paper for the American Society of Mechanical Engineers. His name was Henry Gantt and he titled his paper *A Graphical Daily Balance in Manufacture*. That essay introduced the planning tool of the Gantt Chart.

Gantt's ideas were soon tested on the biggest construction project of that age, the building of the mighty Hoover Dam in Nevada. They used Gantt's technique to plan and control the supply of materials, and to coordinate the complex sequence of tasks and the workforce of over 20,000 people. Opened in 1936, the dam holds back a 180 metre (590ft) high wall of water and stands as an impressive testament to what leaders can achieve through systematic organisation.

Nowadays, Gantt charts are the most widely used graphical method to sequence, organize and control a series of tasks that each depend upon the completion of one or more earlier tasks. And so Henry Gantt became the father of the modern planning and control techniques that combine under the umbrella name of Project Management.

Every major undertaking in the world today uses project management techniques to organise the work and to complete jobs on time, to quality and on budget. People use these techniques on a wide variety of projects that may surprise you such as marketing a new brand of perfume, laying electrical cables, servicing a passenger airplane as quickly and economically as possible, a new musical theatre production, a research project, and many more diverse activities.

Back in 1973, a French engineering company decided to repaint two identical offices. Among their employees was a group of eight graduate trainees. They were young and energetic, fresh from university. They had no experience of painting and decorating and none of them had any training or experience in how to manage a project.

The French company divided the trainees into two teams of four people, Team A and Team B. They gave each team of trainees an identical office to repaint. The teams were given some cash to buy materials. They were told that the ceiling and walls must be washed down and then they must apply two coats of emulsion paint, white for the ceiling and pale cream for the walls. The woodwork must be rubbed down lightly with sandpaper, cleaned using turpentine, painted with one coat of undercoat and a final coat of gloss paint.

The teams were also told to remove the desks, chairs, filing cabinets and other furniture before starting and to replace them afterwards. The teams were not expected to produce a professional standard paint finish but there must be no dabs of paint on the wrong surfaces.

Finally, the teams were told their goal was to repaint the offices as quickly as possible, to the required standard and at the minimum necessary cost.

Both teams immediately voiced how they thought this would be an easy assignment. As one team member said, *'How difficult can it be to paint a room?'* Both teams were completely convinced they could achieve their goal and with a little hard work, they would do the job quickly and to the standard requested.

Team A left the briefing room to make a start. Team B was held back and given some additional instructions. First, they must devote up to two hours planning their work. They must produce a simple written plan in any form they wished, and one team member must be responsible for monitoring progress against the plan.

Team A had already made a start. They were moving furniture and clearing their office.

Team B thought the planning period was overkill for such a simple undertaking but they started to discuss a plan. They had no experience of how to go about this, but then one team member suggested they take a stack of small slips of paper and write one task onto each piece. For example: calculate area to paint, buy sufficient paint, remove desks and chairs, wash walls and ceiling, sand down woodwork, and so on.

The planning process started them thinking in more detail about the sequence of tasks. For example, it made sense to paint the ceiling before the walls, to avoid white paint dripping onto already painted cream-colored walls. They shuffled all these pieces of paper around the desktop into a sequence of activities, working from left to right. The two hours allowed for planning quickly passed so they left their 'plan' on the desktop and started work.

Later that day, the person in Team B tasked with buying the paint read the back of the paint cans and discovered the oil based undercoat used for painting woodwork needed 16 hours to dry, while they could paint over the emulsion paint used for the walls and ceilings after only four hours. He reported that news to the person responsible for monitoring the plan. This lead to rearranging some of the slips of paper on the desktop and amending the order of tasks to make it more likely that by the end of the first day Team B could apply the first coat of paint to the woodwork.

By now, you have probably realised that Team B, with their simple planning and control, was the first to finish. They were four hours quicker and completed painting their office at the end of the second day. Team A had to wait overnight for the undercoat to dry before applying the final topcoat to the woodwork first thing on the third morning. Furthermore, Team B's more careful approach meant they had more accurately calculated the amount of paint required. That meant they had purchased fewer cans of paint, which reduced their costs.

Both teams agreed that next time they had to decorate a room they could do the work quicker and to a higher standard. Such is the value of experience.

'I hear and I forget. I see and I remember. I do and I understand.'
Confucius, 551–479 BC,
Chinese teacher and philosopher.

Redecorating an office has become a common training exercise for teaching the benefits of planning. From that exercise, we can see that an appropriate level of systematic planning and control will save time, help you get it right first time and save money.

'But I don't get involved in projects. My work is different.'

That is a commonly held opinion, and it frequently holds teams back because life invariably becomes easier when we view the work ahead as a project, or a series of projects.

Earlier you read about the project to build the mighty Hoover Dam and the mini-project repainting offices. In both cases, a suitable level of planning and control made a significant difference.

In both of those cases, there was a clearly defined goal that, when completed, signified the end of the job. That fits with this common definition of a project:

> Project: *An individual or collaborative enterprise to achieve a goal, often constrained by objectives for time, quality and cost.*

We should pick that definition apart. When you think about it, everything we do at work is a *'collaborative enterprise to achieve a particular aim.'* For example, if you head a team of social workers your aim will be to improve the quality of life for those you are supporting. That is a specific aim and can have definable target outcomes.

The next part of the project definition states that work is *'often constrained by objectives for time, quality and cost.'* Well, that is usually the case at work. You are very unlikely to be told, *'Take your time, there's no rush'* or *'The quality of your work doesn't matter.'* Everything we do at work must conform to some constraints upon time, resources or quality.

Some work involves repetitive processes that do not at first appear to involve any one-off project work. For example, imagine that you own a small bread bakery. Every day, your team bakes hundreds of loaves of bread. This repetitive process aims to produce thousands of identical loaves, all looking and tasting the same, day after day. That is not a one-off project but a process that your team repeats every day. However, designing, planning and setting up the processes to achieve the daily bread production was a project.

Imagine that a member of your staff leaves your successful small bakery. Now you must recruit and train a suitable new employee. That will be another short project. And then suddenly you face a new challenge, such as the quality of your bread falling, or sales starting to fall, or the price of raw materials rises or a new competing bread shop opens nearby.

In each case you must decide how to respond. Your decision involves change. You will need to find a way to return to a satisfactory situation. You will need to work out how to achieve that goal. That is a plan. And then you must organise your workers to play their part. You will need to encourage and re-motivate your people to rise to the new challenge. Thus, you have a goal, a plan, cost considerations, people and resources to coordinate, which describes a project.

Whenever you need to achieve something new, or to complete a chunk[8] of work to achieve a goal, you will find it becomes much easier if you view it as a project. Just like those trainees who decorated the office, an appropriate amount of planning and systematic organisation speeds up the work,

---

8. Chunk: A manageable, significant, distinct and defined portion of work.

makes it easier to do it right first time and usually saves money. Note that we have spoken of appropriate levels of planning, which I will discuss again later.

Our key point from this chapter is that goals become easier to achieve when viewed as a project.

'First, have a definite, clear practical ideal, a goal, an objective. Second, have the necessary means to achieve your end: wisdom, money, materials, and methods.'

Aristotle, 384–322 BC,
Ancient Greek philosopher, scientist and teacher of
Alexander the Great (356–323).

CHAPTER 3

LEADERS TAKE RESPONSIBILITY FOR MOTIVATING THEIR PEOPLE

It is a curious thing. Aspiring leaders often fail to realise what motivates their people to work for them willingly and enthusiastically.

For a moment, please consider your own motivations. Why do you work?

Is it your need to earn a living, or is it more complex than that? We could list more motivating factors but consider these. Do you feel a need to succeed? Do you crave respect? Are you driven by an altruistic desire to change the world around you? Are power and influence important to you? And there is the question of money. Do you crave greater personal wealth?

Earning a living is the first essential. In fact, many people in the world labour for long and arduous hours, yet barely earn sufficient money to provide themselves with food and shelter. There are even places where both adults and children toil alongside each other for long hours as they perform dangerous manual work. When a person is injured and incapacitated, another desperate person steps forward to take his or her place. The motivation to work comes from a need to survive[9]. The

---

9. At the time of writing, this refers to the conditions of families working at brick kilns in India. If you doubt that such servitude exists today, search the world-wide web and you will surely find other examples.

workers may hate their work but first they must acquire the basics of food and shelter.

On the other hand, some skills are in very short supply, which means that employers must compete to attract staff. Those employers must offer high wages and pleasant working conditions plus extra benefits such as health insurance, longer vacations, etc. Workers who possess expertise that is in high demand are very fortunate. If their boss is unreasonable or just plain incompetent, they have the option to move to an alternative employer.[10]

Once a person's earnings meet their essential cost of living, their motivations change and start to become much more complex. When pay rises above comfort level, and working conditions are pleasant, we look for extra gratification such as the satisfaction of a job well done, team goals achieved, or individual success.

Have you ever considered accepting lower income and reduced financial security in order to gain non-financial rewards? For example, joining an exciting new start-up venture where your personal contribution could play a crucial role in future success. Or perhaps working in a fairly low paid position in a charitable organisation where you can experience the joy of helping.

Once our income is over a certain threshold, we can afford to seek higher motivations than amassing money or expensive vacations, etc. And let us not forget another crucial aspect to motivation, which definitely applies to your team. *To experience job satisfaction, people must be able to succeed...*

This is the pinnacle of motivating desires. For people to experience that fulfilment it must be possible for them to succeed. Employees who are handicapped by poor organisation, inadequate support, no clear direction and other leadership

---

10. At the time of writing, the biggest gap in the developed world between the demand and supply of qualified and experienced people is in information technology. There has been a constant shortage of IT skills since the early 1980s and experts predict this shortage will continue for the foreseeable future.

shortcomings are denied the chance of experiencing full satisfaction.

Thus, capable management and leadership are an essential part of motivating people. The quality of leadership itself can be a strong motivating factor. People will prefer to work for a good leader when other elements, such as pay, might not meet their expectations.

Key Point: *The leader must accept responsibility for motivating the people in his or her team.* In particular, the leader must make it possible for people to experience satisfaction from their work. Later, we will discuss more about how to achieve this. But next we must consider the differing functions of management and leadership.

'True motivation comes from achievement, personal development, job satisfaction, and recognition.'
Frederick Herzberg, 1923–2000,
American psychologist, famous for the
Motivator-Hygiene theory

CHAPTER 4

LEADERSHIP VERSUS MANAGEMENT

As far as this book is concerned, if you head a team of two or more people who must work together to get things done, then you are a leader.

Your formal title might be Executive, Supervisor, Team Leader, Overseer, Controller, Superintendent, Director, Officer, Principal, Manager or many more. But the specific meanings and duties of a leader and a manager are significantly different and need our consideration.

Consider these descriptions:

To Lead:
Guide someone or a group of people, show the way, tend toward a result, escort, pilot, go ahead, direct on a course, conduct.

To Manage:
Run, direct, administer, organise, supervise, deal with, handle, control.

If your team is to get the work done and achieve what it should, then it will require both leadership and management. From the definitions above, we can see that leadership provides the fundamental setting of the direction plus the indispensable guidance, inspiration, and motivation. Your leadership will encourage people to want to deliver their best performance.

But desire alone is not enough. Enthusiasm alone will not achieve very much. You also need to organise and control the sequence of events, to manage. Remove either management or leadership and failure is almost inevitable. Thus, teams cannot accomplish their goals unless their leader provides both the soft skills of leadership and the more systematic skills of management.

- Motivating people, but failing to organise them, usually creates chaos because people do not know exactly what they should be doing.
- Organising and controlling people without motivating them will produce only mediocre performance because although people know what they should do, they will not feel inspired to deliver their best performance.

Your team needs to know how they can do their job. They must understand which tasks to complete today so that they succeed tomorrow, and so on. And you must coordinate each person's work with the efforts of other team members as well as people outside of your team (the wider organisation, customers, suppliers, and other organisations).

Someone must coordinate and manage the work. If you are the Chief Executive of a large organisation, you may choose to focus your own day-to-day actions on formulating strategy rather than providing guidance and inspiration. You can delegate the organisation, supervision and control of detail to other managers.

But if you are the boss of a small company, or a junior or middle manager within a large organisation, or if you lead a team at the sharp end of achieving results, you may not have the option to delegate the management to somebody else. In which case, you must adopt the roles of both manager and leader. Your job description then includes guidance, inspiration, direction, administration, organisation, supervision, monitoring progress, support and an appropriate level of control.

Let there be no misunderstanding, it is the leader's responsibility to either provide the management or have somebody else do it for them. If you can provide the leadership and delegate the management to someone else, that is fine. But if there is nobody available to provide that management, you have no choice but to step in and fulfil both roles. For you, the adage applies, *'If it is going to be, it's up to me.'*[11]

'Management is about arranging and telling. Leadership is about nurturing and enhancing.'

> *Thomas J. Peters, b1942, co-author of In Search of Excellence (1982).*

---

11. Copyright Brian Tracey: *The Psychology of Achievement:The Phoenix Seminar* (Nightingale-Conant Corporation, 1986)

CHAPTER 5

YOUR TEAM TENDS TO LIVE UP OR DOWN TO YOUR EXPECTATIONS

We observe our team members at work and intuitively form opinions about them. We cannot help but do that. It is an instinct that is hard wired into all of us[12].

Now consider three questions:

- How willing are your people?
- Do they work hard or are they either demotivated or lazy?
- If necessary, will your co-workers go the extra mile to complete the job?

Please do that now...

Continue reading after you have answered the above three questions.

No doubt, you based answers to those questions upon knowledge of your team in general and your views on particular personalities. Was your judgement of your people generally

---

12. For detailed academic reading on this subject, check out the work of Professor Frank Bernieri of Oregon State University who coined the phrase 'thin-slicing methodology' to describe how we instinctively form opinions from small snippets of observation.

good or bad? Let us hope it was good, because your opinion makes a difference.

For a start, even if you hold your opinions close to your chest and try not to reveal them, you will surely let slip indicators which betray what you really think.[13] People are sensitive to any wording that betrays a difference between what we truly think and what we say. And people often notice when our body language implies a different meaning to our words. People also pick up on how you treat them compared to how you treat others. If you think your people are not up to the job, then you had best prepare for disappointment because people tend to perform poorly when expectations are low. Several well-regarded studies have observed this effect, called the *'Golem Effect.'*[14]

Likewise, positive expectations lift results. This phenomenon is difficult to study in the workplace because one cannot isolate the effect from all the other influences upon performance. However, in 1963, Robert Rosenthal and Lenore Jacobson illustrated this effect when they conducted a study of children at school. The study showed that if you lead teachers to expect an enhanced performance from children, then those children improve their performance.[15] And consider this…

Just as you observe your people and form opinions about their capability, they also watch you and form opinions about your ability to lead them. If your team does not rate you highly it will very probably have the effect of reducing your personal performance. Poor expectations can easily become a self-fulfilling prophecy, with negativity infecting all concerned. So, how do you prevent this?

---

13. Among many research papers, this one discusses more subtle body language: *Body Cues, Not Facial Expressions, Discriminate Between Intense Positive and Negative Emotions*, by Aviezer, Trope and Todorov, 2012
14. The effect is named after Golem, a clay creature in Jewish mythology. Major Wilburn Schrank demonstrated the Golem Effect as far back as 1968, when he carried out an experiment on students at the United States Airforce Academy.
15. Named The Pygmalion Effect (Greek myth of Pygmalion) or Rosenthal Effect (Rosenthal–Jacobson study, 1963)

Genuinely thinking the best of your people is an important foundation for success. Whenever possible, foster within yourself positive opinions of your workmates' abilities. For example, when appropriate you might comment, *'I knew you could do it.'* Look for opportunities to catch people doing well and take the opportunity to praise them for their efforts. A ratio of three praises to one criticism[16] should be the absolute minimum because people tend to remember our negative remarks more readily than our positive comments.

When members of your team rise to the occasion, everyone wins. And when, despite your encouragement, a person falls short, you will think about it, decide what to do, and then act appropriately.

'There is an English proverb that says there are no bad students, only bad teachers. I believe it also applies to a company. There are no bad employees, only bad managers.'
> *Dr. T.S. Lin, 1918–2006, CEO of Tatung*
> *Company for 30 years*

---

16. The critical positivity ratio (the Losada ratio) is probably not founded upon sound research. However, the author's experience supports the idea this is a sensible minimum when managing/leading people.

CHAPTER 6

BELIEF VERSUS SYSTEMATIC ORGANISATION

We have established that…
- … Belief is essential to our success.
- … Planning and organisation make it much easier to achieve our goals.

Those two facts are equally important. However, they can, on occasion, appear to be opposing viewpoints. Therefore, we will now consider a core challenge that all leaders must face and conquer, namely that barring miracles some things must be just plain impossible to achieve. No amount of positive thinking will magically convert them from unattainable to attainable.

So, how can we know if our belief is flying in the face of reality? And how do we avoid sabotaging our ability to achieve the more difficult challenges by not fostering a positive attitude? When is belief a positive force for success and when does it tempt us to foolishly expend much of our energy, time, money and other resources pursuing a fool's errand?

Many leaders have trouble with that dichotomy. Some plough on, relying on the view that belief eventually conquers all. In some cases that may be true, but the key word eventually could mean long after the intended completion date and at a much higher cost than is acceptable.

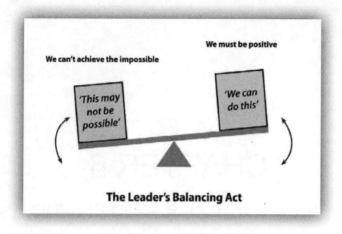

We can't achieve the impossible

We must be positive

'This may not be possible'

'We can do this'

The Leader's Balancing Act

When pondering these matters, leaders often fall into two camps, which reflect their own personal preferred leadership style. Around half focus all their energy on promoting the idea that *'We can do this,'* the emotional approach to leadership. Meanwhile, the other half concentrate upon analysing the work ahead: *'Let us determine if and how we could do this,'* which is the systematic approach to leadership.

We already know that both approaches are valid and necessary. Right now, you may well be leaning towards your own natural preference for systems and organisation or for a less formal but confident and positive approach.

What if you could have it all?

There is a world-beating example of the benefits of combining both schools of thought, emotional and systematic. This example is astonishing because of the breathtaking boldness of the goal and the extreme difficulty of the task.

On September 12 1962, the President of the USA, John F. Kennedy, rose to speak at Rice University in Texas. As always, the media filmed his speech for worldwide distribution – you can easily find it online. President Kennedy astonished the world when he committed his country to, within eight years, sending men to the moon and bringing them back alive – the Apollo Mission. In 1962 this was the stuff of science fiction.

Top space scientists considered it would eventually be possible to land men on the moon, but not for some years. There were huge problems to overcome, which Kennedy acknowledged in his speech:

> *'We shall send men to the moon, 240,000 miles away from the control station in Houston, a giant rocket more than 300 feet tall, the length of this football field, made of new metal alloys, some of which have not yet been invented, capable of standing heat and stresses several times more than have ever been experienced, fitted together with a precision better than the finest watch, carrying all the equipment needed for propulsion, guidance, control, communications, food and survival, on an untried mission, to an unknown celestial body, and then return it safely to earth, re-entering the atmosphere at speeds of over 25,000 miles per hour, causing heat about half that of the temperature of the sun...and do all this, and do it right, and do it first before this decade is out...'*

Kennedy's speech left no doubt that everyone concerned was irrevocably committed to success, which really focussed the minds of all involved. Next, over the coming months, the President met with many of the scientists, engineers and project leaders. He whipped up a belief that it could and would be done. This was not fantasy. Kennedy had previously researched space travel carefully and satisfied himself the project was possible. All he was doing was to force the pace of discovery and progress.

Note that Kennedy made an absolute commitment to a defined goal. He then convincingly displayed his total belief in success. The leaders in command of the project transmitted that belief down the chain of command to infect and inspire everyone who worked upon the project.

Would the Apollo Mission have succeeded without that commitment? It would probably have not, because a lack of dedication saps energy and creativity. The German philosopher Goethe put it this way :

> *'There is one element of truth, the ignorance of which kills countless ideas and splendid plans. From the moment that one definitely commits oneself providence moves too. All sorts of things occur to help one that would never otherwise have occurred. A whole stream of events issues from the decision, raising in one's favour all manner of unforeseen incidents and meetings and material assistance which no man could have dreamed would have come his way.'*

The greatest achievements in history all started with a definite commitment. The building of the pyramids of Egypt, the Great Wall of China and many other ventures all started with an absolute steadfastness that *'We shall do this!'* However, a gung-ho attitude alone did not build the pyramids or the Great Wall. Commitment undeniably raised levels of energy and creativity but archaeologists have uncovered evidence that those ancient projects involved sophisticated levels of systematic organisation and administration which coordinated all the innumerable pieces of detail.

As you know, men did reach the moon. Twelve men walked on the moon between 1969 and 1972. Now we fast forward twenty years, to when the American National Aeronautics and Space Agency (NASA) brought together six experts to evaluate the legacy of the Apollo Mission.[17] Their report concluded that:

---

17. *Managing the Moon Program: Lessons Learned from Project Apollo, Proceedings of an Oral History Workshop Conducted July 21, 1989.* Published by NASA and available online.

'It may be that the most lasting legacy of Apollo was human: an improved understanding of how to plan, coordinate and monitor the myriad technical activities that were the building blocks of Apollo... NASA personnel employed a program management concept that centralised authority over design, engineering, procurement, testing, construction, manufacturing, spare parts, logistics, training, and operations.'

And the American Association for the Advancement of Science observed the following:

'In terms of complexity, rate of growth and technological sophistication it has been unique... it may turn out that the space program's most valuable spin-off of all will be human rather than technological: better knowledge of how to plan, coordinate and monitor the multitudinous and varied activities...'

The Apollo mission combined six elements that together create a perfect storm of productivity and increase the likelihood of achieving any goal, including yours, no matter how small or large:

- Clearly defined goal
- Commitment to success
- Inspiring leadership
- Shared belief in success
- Planning
- Organisation and coordination of people and resources

Those six elements combine the power of belief with the skills of systematic planning and organisation.

Employ all six components and you significantly improve the likelihood of success. Ignore just one and you handicap your team. Do you agree? Let us hope so. But for some people, their inner preference towards being either an emotional motivator or a calculating systemiser is so strong that it leads them astray. Beware of that natural inclination, which exists within all of us, one way or the other.

At this point, it is possible that some readers might be thinking 'I cannot see myself as a motivational personality,' or 'I'm not cut out to be a nitty-gritty details and systems person.'

If you think either of the above, park those thoughts at the back of your mind for now, because in part two of this book you will read how anyone can lead their team by combining belief and commitment with systematic organisation.

'It takes less work to succeed than to fail. Put another way: failure means you have worked hard for nothing! With less work, directed systematically, you would have succeeded.'
W Clement Stone, 1902–2002
American businessperson and philanthropist
who rose from poverty to riches, and according
to the New York Times 'built an empire on optimism'.

KEY POINTS SO FAR

- It is a myth that leaders are born.
- Leadership requires positive action. The leadership sequence is: learn, think, decide, act.
- With application, almost anyone can become an exceptionally good leader. The transformation from average to outstanding can be astonishingly fast.
- Perception is the gatekeeper to results. People rarely accomplish things they do not believe they can achieve.
- Goals become easier to achieve when viewed as a project.
- Leaders take responsibility for motivating their people. Leaders continuously make it easier for team members to want to achieve things for their leader.
- Leadership alone is not enough, management is also essential. Leadership provides the essential motivation to strive for success and management provides the essential organisation to make it possible.
- Your team will tend to live up or down to your expectations. It pays to hold positive expectations of your people.
- Belief, commitment and systematic organisation combine to enable people to <u>truly</u> believe that *'We can do this...'* That combination provides people with the means to succeed.

The Five Modes of Leadership

In a perfect world, we would lead people by acting in a sequence of modes, as above. First, in <u>vision</u> mode, we would decide a goal. We would <u>plan</u> how to achieve our goal and then <u>delegate</u> the work. Next, we would ensure everything is running smoothly and thereby <u>enable</u> people to succeed. After those steps, everything would progress so smoothly that we could <u>empower</u> our people to do the work without any more work on our part. We would be free to turn our attention elsewhere, confident that our team will work effectively on their own and achieve our goal.

CHAPTER 7

INTRODUCING THE FIVE MODES OF LEADERSHIP

To introduce the Five Modes of Leadership, let us first consider leading a group of people who work to achieve a goal in which everything goes perfectly. The team performs excellently and there are no unforeseen challenges to address. In that case we would act in a sequence of leadership modes[18] as illustrated, like this:

- **Vision Mode**

  You decide your <u>vision</u> for the future. You set a goal that you can see clearly in your mind's eye. Your goal is clearly defined, which means that success is measurable. You know the criteria for determining success so you will know for sure when you have achieved your goal. Achieving your goal may require hard work, skill and coping with some uncertainty, but you believe the goal to be feasible[19]. Some leaders get to decide their own goals and others need to accept the goals that are set for them.

---

18. Mode: A possible, customary, or preferred way of doing something. A way of behaving, especially one that becomes instinctive, familiar, or habitual. (From Oxford English Dictionary)

19. Feasible: Possible and practical to do or achieve. (From Oxford English Dictionary)

- **Plan Mode**

  You <u>plan</u> how the work will be done. You, or more likely yourself and suitable people in your team, define the few critical and most important milestones[20] that you must achieve along the way to completion. You decide what tasks must be completed to achieve each milestone. You arrange all the tasks and milestones into a sensible sequence as you figure out what must be done, and who will do the work. Now you have a plan, which enables you to believe more strongly in forthcoming success.

- **Delegate Mode**

  You <u>delegate</u> tasks and things start to happen. People see the vision start to become reality. The team starts to make progress, which helps to increase their belief that the goal is possible to achieve.

- **Enable Mode**

  You <u>enable</u> individuals and groups of people to succeed by making sure each person will not be held back in any way through lack of skills, knowledge, materials, methods, outside support and so on. You coordinate the work between people. This is when team members really experience your effective leadership at first hand. They feel fully engaged in the process of achieving the goals.

- **Empower Mode**

  Everything is progressing as planned. The work is on schedule and to the standard required. Some, perhaps even all, your people are capable of completing their tasks and achieving their individual objectives without your input or control. You can now <u>empower</u>[21] those

---

20. Milestone: A significant stage or event to mark points of progress during a project. For example, milestones could include project start and end, a point for external review, the completion of one type of work, and other major progress points that must be reached to achieve the end goal.

21. Empower: Give someone the authority or power to do something. Make someone stronger and more confident, especially in controlling their life. (Oxford English Dictionary)

people to take full command of themselves and their work. Most people find this to be liberating and motivating. In this mode of working, people tend to deliver their highest levels of personal productivity. And when they contribute to work that reaches or expands their potential ability, they feel good about themselves. They may even achieve the highest level of motivation and fulfilment, which the psychologist Abraham Maslow called 'self-actualisation'[22].

LEADERSHIP IS USUALLY LESS WELL-ORDERED

The description above explains the Five Modes of Leadership in the sequence of Vision, Plan, Delegate, Enable and Empower.

Very occasionally, a chunk of work will progress in that well-ordered fashion. However, we generally find that life at work does not progress exactly as planned. We may have to lead our team through disordered and even chaotic periods. This means the leader needs to become adept at switching back and forth between the modes as we cope with changing circumstances. For example, how often have you experienced the following setbacks?

- Team members who may be skilled and experienced often do not act as we expect.
- Outside influences conspire to sabotage progress.
- Suppliers let us down.
- Bosses change the objectives after we have started.
- Customers modify their requirements.

---

22. Abraham Maslow (1908-1970), American psychologist who created *Maslow's Hierarchy of Needs*, a theory of human needs and fulfilment culminating in self-actualisation, which can be defined as: the realisation or fulfilment of one's talents and potentialities, a drive or need that is present in everyone.

And communications between people sometimes go wrong. The leader may unknowingly be the cause of this. For example, they explain what he or she wants done and thinks people have fully understood the instructions when they have not.

The leader thinks the worker will do what is required of him or her. But instead, to the leader's complete surprise, the worker does what they believe to be correct, but it is something entirely different from what the leader wanted.

Poor communication between people is probably the most common root cause for work not progressing as desired. And that assumes the plan was flawless in the first place, which is rarely the case. Also, perceptions and attitudes will either boost or handicap progress.

When we harbour doubts about whether our team can complete some piece of work, despite efforts to appear positive, we unconsciously communicate our misgivings. Team members will likely respond with a less than committed performance. In effect, they live down to our negative expectations and thus our personal doubts have sabotaged progress. However, there is also good news...

When you employ the right mode of leadership for each situation you minimise the potential for those things to go wrong. You act in the most appropriate way for each situation and thus maximise the probability of success.

THE FIVE MODES OF LEADERSHIP WILL HELP YOU TO LEAD PEOPLE IN THE 'REAL' WORLD

The most capable leaders, without consciously thinking about it, will frequently switch between one or more of the Five Modes of Leadership. The rest of us need to inject a little extra thought as we select the most appropriate mode of leadership for every situation.

DECIDING WHICH MODE OF LEADERSHIP TO ADOPT

On the next page you will see the Five Modes of Leadership: Vision, Plan, Delegate, Enable, Empower. The leader usually commences each new goal in Vision mode. This is when the new idea becomes a clearly defined chunk of work that is written down as your goal, and you check the goal is feasible. Frankly, there is little point in progressing further until you have reasonable confidence that it is possible to attain this goal.

The modes of Plan, Delegate and Enable may occasionally be sequential but you will usually find it necessary to switch between these modes according to circumstances, varying your leadership style to match the situation, the person, the group of people, the type of work, and changing circumstances.

You select the relevant and most effective mode of leadership for each set of circumstances. How do you do that? Everything will become clear in the next few chapters.

Of course, leading people will not suddenly become easy. You will still need to be self-disciplined, self-controlled, think carefully, be determined and work hard. However, people quickly respond to positive and directed leadership, which in turn gives you a high return for the effort you invest.

The Five Modes of Leadership

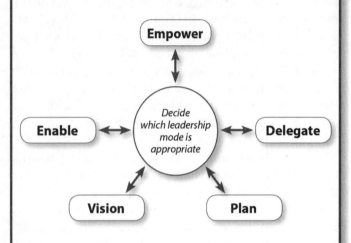

You adopt the appropriate mode of leadership for the situation. As you lead your team you will switch back and forth between modes, matching your approach to the circumstances. And you may often select different modes for leading different people.

PART TWO

START TO EMPLOY
THE FIVE MODES OF LEADERSHIP
FOR REAL

'The mode by which the inevitable happens is effort.'
Oliver Wendell Holmes, 1809–1894,
American physician and professor at Harvard University.

'There is an objective reality out there, but we always view it through the lens of our beliefs and values.'

David G. Myers, BA, MA, PhD, b1942,
Professor of Psychology, Hope College, USA

CHAPTER 8

SELECT A CURRENT GOAL

To benefit from reading this book you must take action. Having read and absorbed the content so far, you are ready.

Do not focus upon the many objectives[23] you may currently be working upon but only your end goals[24]. You need a written list, so if that is not already available, quickly write a list of your current goals.

Review your goal list, which should contain a number of clearly defined outcomes. If you have only one goal on your list, that means you have the advantage of focussing all your attention upon achieving one outcome.

If your list has more than one goal, you need to select one. This will be the first goal upon which you start employing the Five Modes of Leadership. Perhaps this should be your team's single most important goal, which when achieved, will have the greatest positive impact upon your future success.

Pause reading and select one goal right now...

Now you have chosen, turn to the next chapter and consider the Leader's Perception.

---

23. Objective: One of possibly many definable outcomes or measures of progress needed to achieve the goal referred to above.
24. Goal: The desired end outcome from a chunk of work.

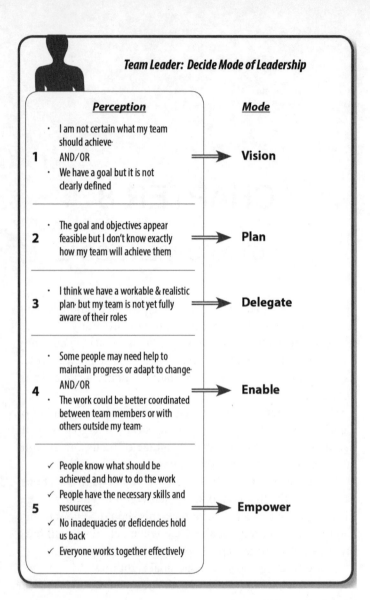

Team Leader: Decide Mode of Leadership

	Perception		*Mode*
1	· I am not certain what my team should achieve· AND/OR · We have a goal but it is not clearly defined	⟹	**Vision**
2	· The goal and objectives appear feasible but I don't know exactly how my team will achieve them	⟹	**Plan**
3	· I think we have a workable & realistic plan· but my team is not yet fully aware of their roles	⟹	**Delegate**
4	· Some people may need help to maintain progress or adapt to change· AND/OR · The work could be better coordinated between team members or with others outside my team·	⟹	**Enable**
5	✓ People know what should be achieved and how to do the work ✓ People have the necessary skills and resources ✓ No inadequacies or deficiencies hold us back ✓ Everyone works together effectively	⟹	**Empower**

CHAPTER 9

CONSIDER YOUR
PERCEPTIONS

In chapter one, you read how *perception is the gatekeeper to results*. That fundamental truth reveals a key to deciding which of the Five Modes of Leadership will enable you and your team to deliver peak performance in any given situation. It works like this:

1. You consider your personal perceptions.
2. You use those insights to indicate which mode of leadership to adopt.
3. The chosen mode of leadership will help you determine what actions to take.

In the previous chapter, you chose a current goal. Consider your goal and the work ahead. Read the five alternative groups of perceptions in the diagram opposite.

Which of those descriptions most closely describes your likelihood of achieving your goal on time, to the standard required, and where relevant, for the target cost? Select one of the five options. If you find you want to select two groups of perception descriptions, select the lowest numbered option. For example, if you are not sure how your team can achieve the goal (Perception 2) or if the goal is actually clearly defined (Perception 1), then select the lowest numbered option, which in that case would be Perception 1. When you have your answer, continue reading.

Was your decision made quickly or after considered analysis? We all have a natural preference for how we make decisions. Our preference is explained by one of the many facets of our personality. The result is that some of us tend to make quicker decisions than others. The decision you just made is an indicator of which type of decision maker you are.

Knowing and understanding your own personality is very useful to a leader because often you will need to do what must be done instead of what you prefer to do or what comes naturally. What does that mean for you?

You will find that somewhere in this book you will read one or more suggested actions that would not come naturally for you. Therefore, you will instinctively want to avoid adopting the suggestion. When that happens, it would be wise to ask yourself, 'Is my reluctance because the suggested action wants me to act out of my comfort zone, or personality type? And should I therefore be prepared to overcome my reluctance and try the suggestion?'[25].

We should take a step sideways for a minute to consider the two alternative types of decision making – considered versus quick – because they may produce different answers.

Has your gut feeling ever told you not to do something when your more considered opinion was to go ahead? Have you ever done something, or held back from doing something against your gut feeling, and then afterwards wished you had listened to your small inner voice? It is very likely you have experienced those feelings.

Psychologists who study 'gut feeling' versus 'considered decisions' now describe instant decisions as resulting from 'thin slice' thinking. There is mounting evidence that thin slice thinking can be more reliable than pondering a decision for a

---

25. If this area interests you, you could learn more about your personality type by completing a Myers Briggs survey. Free surveys and results are available on the web, e.g: www.teamtechnology.co.uk

longer time[26]. Unsurprisingly, there is also evidence that our gut feeling is most reliable when we consider issues that are within our area of expertise[27].

Not long ago, management experts considered it reckless to respect our gut feeling. In 2003, the Harvard Business Review published an article titled *'Don't trust your gut.'* Then, just nine years later, in 2012, that same worthy publication printed another article proposing the exact opposite, that *'Instinct can beat analytical thinking.'* This reflects recent research into thin sliced thinking. There is one important stipulation: thin sliced opinions on subjects about which we have little or no knowledge are unlikely to be accurate. But when it comes to your area of expertise and experience, then research shows that your gut feeling is a valid and important indicator.

Returning to your goal: to confirm, this is not a theoretical exercise. You are considering an important goal for you and your team. You need to choose one of the five alternatives in the diagram on page 66. If you wavered between two descriptions, perhaps because your gut feeling came up with a different answer to your considered opinion, then you should prefer the lower numbered option. That will be most prudent, because it will avoid you missing any essential actions.

Once you have chosen which of the perceptions most closely matches your situation, you can turn to the relevant chapter for the indicated leadership mode, as in the following diagram:

---

26. 'Thin slice judgments are intuitive. These judgments are efficient: They do not seem to drain cognitive resources and can be accurate even when processed in parallel with other tasks.' *The Perils of Pondering: Intuition and Thin Slice Judgments* by Nalini Ambady, Department of Psychology, Tufts University, Medford, Massachusetts, 2010

27. 'The effectiveness of intuition relative to analysis is amplified at a high level of domain expertise.' *When should I trust my gut? Linking domain expertise to intuitive decision-making effectiveness, by* Dane, Rockman & Pratt, from Organizational Behavior and Human Decision Processes 119(2);187-194, 2012.

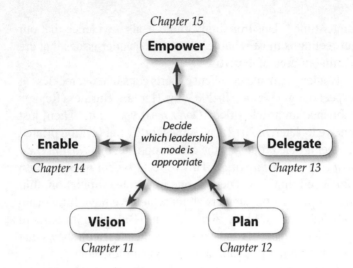

Chapter 15
Empower

Enable
Chapter 14

Decide which leadership mode is appropriate

Delegate
Chapter 13

Vision
Chapter 11

Plan
Chapter 12

However, it pays to think about how things look from your team members' standpoint. After all, your people are the ones who will do the work. Their perceptions have a crucial effect upon whether you attain any goal. To consider team members' perceptions, read the next chapter.

'Attitude is a little thing that makes a big difference.'
Winston Churchill, 1874–1965,
twice Prime Minister of the UK,
most notably during World War II.
Winner of the Nobel Prize for Literature, 1953

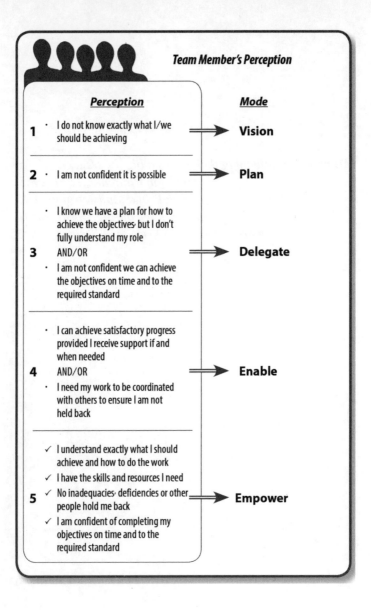

Team Member's Perception

Perception		*Mode*
1 · I do not know exactly what I/we should be achieving	⟹	**Vision**
2 · I am not confident it is possible	⟹	**Plan**
3 · I know we have a plan for how to achieve the objectives, but I don't fully understand my role AND/OR · I am not confident we can achieve the objectives on time and to the required standard	⟹	**Delegate**
4 · I can achieve satisfactory progress provided I receive support if and when needed AND/OR · I need my work to be coordinated with others to ensure I am not held back	⟹	**Enable**
5 ✓ I understand exactly what I should achieve and how to do the work ✓ I have the skills and resources I need ✓ No inadequacies, deficiencies or other people hold me back ✓ I am confident of completing my objectives on time and to the required standard	⟹	**Empower**

CHAPTER 10

CONSIDER EACH TEAM MEMBER'S PERCEPTIONS

It is wise to consider each team member's view on the likelihood of success for the following reasons:

- If your people do not believe in forthcoming success, they will be severely handicapped and you need to know that.
- If your people feel confident, despite your personal misgivings, you need to understand why your people see things differently.
- Some of your people may be more knowledgeable than yourself in certain areas. Their opinions can be very valuable. The larger their bank of knowledge and experience, the more you need their opinion.
- Some of your team may be less capable of doing the work than you currently think. Those people may or may not be aware of their deficiencies. You may be able to work around that handicap, but only if you know.
- A member of your team may think that *'It cannot be done'* and be correct. If someone has good reason to know your goal is impossible, you need to know. You may need to change your approach, modify the goal or find some way around the problem. But first, you need to know.

If you lead a large organisation with several tiers of management between you and the people who do the work, you need to consider the perceptions of your core team of senior managers. In turn, they should consider their own team, and so on down the organisation. You want an organisation where the perceptions of front-line people are communicated to you as quickly as possible.

To gather team members' perceptions, you could ask each person directly, but you may not always receive a straightforward answer. They may tailor their reply to what they think you want to hear. Or they may be reluctant to impart bad news and soften the message so much that you cannot decipher the true meaning. How open and honest people are will depend upon their personal confidence and the culture of the organisation.

Which of these statements by junior people most accurately describes the culture within your organisation?

- A. 'I enjoy my work, it can be rewarding. The team focusses on results, getting the job done. We all support team success. My opinion is valued.'
- B. 'People do not always cooperate with each other when they could or should. I am not sure how my work contributes to the overall picture. If I were to speak out I might suffer consequences.'

If you work in a place like A above, your people should feel they can share their honest opinions with you. They know you will accept and welcome whatever they have to say.

If you work in an organisation more like B above, your people may be reluctant to tell you what they really think. This is a counterproductive culture which makes it harder for you to succeed. You will need to change the culture within your team. It is the leader's job to create an effective culture in his or her team. In fact, 'If leaders do not create the culture they want, they get a culture they definitely don't want.'[28]

You can quickly improve communication within your team if you set the example. Demonstrate that people can give you their opinion and receive approval rather than criticism or disdain. You do not have to agree with what people say but you can let them know you heard what they said and would rather they had voiced their opinion than kept quiet. When you remove the fear of negative consequences people start to 'tell it like it is.'

Over time, as you lead your team using the Five Modes of Leadership, you will engender a very productive culture including better communication between team members.

And now back to the immediate need for you to learn team members' perceptions. Do the following:

- Ask your most senior team members straight out. Take their instant thin sliced view. For the people who find it hard to give an immediate opinion, allow them a little more time to deliver their considered opinion. You could show them the Team Member's Perception diagram, or you could listen to their words and then translate them into which one of the five boxes in the diagram most closely matches their answer.

- Canvass opinions directly from more junior team members. Workers love it when senior leaders take an interest in their work and views. It shows how you value them. You can do this as directly or as subtly as suits your own communication style. Be careful to retain the support of any middle managers as you do that.

Divide the opinions you receive from this group into two sets:

1. Team members with applicable expertise. Their opinion is most valuable.

---

28. This refers to Law 26, from *The Secret Laws of Management*, by the author (Published by Headline Business Plus)

2. Those who have less expertise or experience and could be considered less qualified to express an opinion. On occasion, their lack of experience could produce unbiased and valuable insights.

Continually be aware of the true meaning of all conversation at work. You may already be expert at interpreting people's words, though this is an area where we can always benefit from learning more. Listen attentively and notice the subtleties of conversation. This is where, without asking, people reveal their true thoughts. A simple example that you will have experienced follows:

When given new work, some people will say, '*I'll try.*' That phrase should ring alarm bells because it is often the precursor to disappointment. To avoid telling you the hard truth, '*I cannot do that,*' people may let you down more gradually. First, you hear, '*I will try,*' then, '*I tried,*' and finally '*I warned you I might not be able to do that.*'

At work, many people will choose to modify their wording to avoid conflict or appear agreeable. They do this by making ambiguous statements using words that listeners can interpret in more than one way. We all do this to some extent. It is part of normal social life.

This way of communicating is ingrained in society and is not going to change, which complicates life for the leader. You need plain facts upon which to base decisions. This means you must be skilled at teasing out the real meaning behind what people say.[29]

People also communicate their true feelings with non-verbal signs or body language, which confirms or betrays their words. Our bodies reveal our true thoughts whilst our mouths voice something completely different. For example,

29. For an academic study into this effect, read *Talking Heads: Language, Met-alanguage, and the Semiotics of Subjectivity* by Benjamin Lee (Duke University Press, 1997). For a lighter read: *Talk Language* by Allan Pease & Alan Garner (Orion Books, 2002).

'*I am really keen on this idea*' sounds supportive, but if the speaker stands with arms folded and hunched shoulders their body language disagrees with their words. Body language falls outside the scope of this book, but if you have not recently done so, bringing your knowledge of body language up to date is highly recommended[30].

Now, consider your current goal and team member perceptions related to that goal. Which of the five perceptions in the diagram from page 72 most closely matches your team's opinion? If you are undecided between two boxes, choose the lower numbered choice.

Having selected the mode indicated, the diagram on the next page indicates which chapter to read next, when we will consider that mode of leadership.

'Listen more than you talk. Nobody learned anything by hearing themselves speak.'

Sir Richard Branson, b 1950, English business magnate and philanthropist, founder of the Virgin Group, which controls more than 400 companies.

---

30. Body language: The conscious and unconscious movements and postures by which attitudes and feelings are communicated (Oxford English Dictionary). Suggested further reading: *The Definitive Book of Body Language: How to read others' attitudes by their gestures* by Allan & Barbara Pease (Orion Books, 2006).

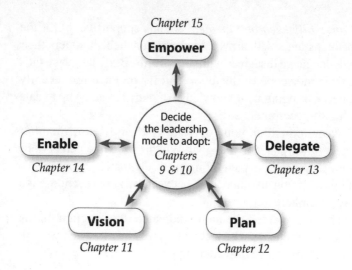

'We should listen carefully to the views of the cadres[31] at the lowest levels. Be a pupil before you become a teacher, learn from the cadres at the lower levels before you issue orders.'

Mao Tse-tung, 1893–1976,
1st Chairman of the People's Republic of China.

---

31. Cadre: A small group of people specially trained for a particular purpose or profession, a group of activists in a communist or other revolutionary organisation (Oxford English Dictionary).

PART THREE

APPLY THE FIVE MODES OF LEADERSHIP

Option One:
You could read the following chapters straight through, in sequence.

Option Two:
You will gain the maximum by immediately employing the appropriate mode of leadership on the current goal you selected in Chapter 8. If you have not already done so, read Chapters 9 and 10 to select the mode of leadership and then read the relevant chapter, as indicated by the diagram on the opposite page.

CHAPTER 11

LEADERSHIP MODE VISION

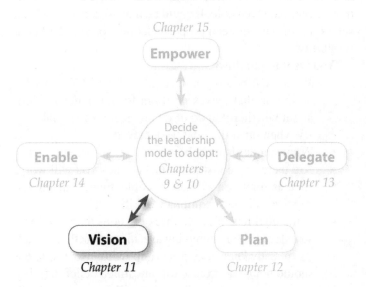

Objectives in Vision Mode:
- Have a clearly defined goal because you can only achieve a goal when you know exactly what it is.
- You believe it is feasible within an acceptable degree of certainty that you and your team can achieve the goal in the timescale required, to the agreed standard and with the resources you have available (labour, skills, materials, time available, outside support, etc.)
- You have created a vision of the goal which will help you to enthuse and motivate others.

Act in Vision mode when you are not certain what you and your team should achieve and when you are not confident that a new goal is feasible. It could be that no goals have been set, or a goal has not been properly defined, or you doubt the feasibility.

You want to pin down:
- What exactly are you trying to achieve? You need a definition that leaves no room for misunderstanding about whether you do or do not achieve the goal.
- By when must the goal be achieved?
- What standards must be met?
- Are there any constraints under which you will work, such as limits on available people, money, materials, support, services, equipment, skills, etc?
- Is the goal feasible? On rare occasions there will be a sound reason for attempting to achieve something which you already know may prove impossible. However, that should not be an excuse for unjustified belief in trying to achieve the impossible. You will generally want to know that a goal is at least possible before you start investing your time, money, effort and reputation.

You need to be certain about what is required so that when your team achieves the goal, everyone will be able to agree upon completion and celebrate success. And you do not want to attain your goal to later discover that other people were expecting you to achieve something different, which happens more often than one might expect.

Beware of ill-defined or shifting goals because they usually lead to disappointment. Attempting to achieve them would be like your boss telling you to walk to a place but not giving you the correct name for the destination or pointing it out on the map. You might assume you know where you are going but you would not be sure. You could not plan how long it will take or what you need for the journey. And imagine that after you have travelled some distance your boss contacts you and changes your target. Sound crazy? Well, all too often bosses require teams to work at ill-defined or shifting goals that waste resources, ensure failure and demoralise people. Beware!

If other people set your goals, this does not mean you simply agree to any ill-defined destination set for you. Just as you need to take account of your team members' perceptions, your boss must consider yours. You need to be able to tell him or her with conviction that, *'I understand exactly what you want me to achieve.'* The best way to be certain of that is to define goals in writing. If necessary, write that definition yourself and then agree the detail with your boss. If you compromise on this point you will almost certainly regret it later. Starting with a clear vision of the end destination is the starting point for success.

THE IMPORTANCE OF TEAM MEMBERS' PERCEPTIONS

If team members think they don't know exactly what they should be doing the reason could be that:
1. You have not set a goal that provides work for them to do.
2. You have not communicated your delegation clearly.
3. There is a hidden reason for their views.

In case 1 above the solution is to set goals and start delegating work. In case 2 you need to review your delegation and re-delegate the work more clearly. Chapter 12 discusses delegation in detail.

In case 3 above you need to uncover the hidden reasons. Sometimes at work people hide their real thoughts behind unclear use of language, or make misleading statements.

For example, when a person feels incapable of doing the work he or she might not tell you straight out that *'I can't do this.'* Instead you may hear statements such as, *'I don't know what is expected of me'* or *'Someone else should do this,'* or *'Right now I am so busy I can't take on extra work.'* These are avoidance strategies that prevent the boss from getting a true understanding of what the person is really thinking.

Avoidance strategies may indicate you have a culture problem. If people think that making a negative comment would be a problem, they will avoid saying anything that may lead to them receiving criticism.

If people receive a negative or critical response from their boss when they tell it like it is, or at least how they see things, then people start using avoidance language. They may try to make their point in a roundabout way. They may try to shift blame elsewhere. They may become skilled at avoiding doing any work that might fail. All of which is counter-productive and makes life for the leader difficult.

Have you already created an effective culture within your team? If not, you need to do so because *'When leaders do not create the culture they want, they get a culture they definitely don't want'*[32]. The most effective leaders create an open and no-nonsense culture where anyone can 'tell it like it is' and not be put down with blame or criticism. Your focus always remains upon positive solutions and moving forwards and you always require the same from your team.

---

32. More detail on this subject in Law 26 in *The Secret Laws of Management*, by the author, published in 2010.

Thus, when people say they do not know what they should be doing, calmly respond as an effective leader. Remove that uncertainty and if the problem with their attitude remains, you know there are hidden reason for their negative stance. Dig for the reason. You will learn things to your advantage.

Unfortunately, a few people just love being negative and making unreasonable and incorrect negative statements. If those people will not change and join your positive, pragmatic culture, they must go.

SUMMARY OF ACTIONS IN VISION MODE

1. Clearly define the goal.
2. Where relevant, make sure team members understand the goal.
3. Check it is feasible for you and your team to achieve the goal in the timescale, to the required standard and using available resources.
4. Write a vision that you can share, displaying your genuine enthusiasm and conviction.

Next, we consider each of those steps in more detail.

DEFINE THE GOAL

First, you must do this with no loose descriptions that may become the first step toward failure. Write goals precisely so that everyone concerned can agree the aims, beyond doubt. Use words that can only describe one intended outcome. JF Kennedy was very specific: *'We shall send men to the moon and then return them safely before this decade is out.'* That's the way to do it: concise, exact, specific, time bound and measurable.

CHECK FEASIBILITY

Considering feasibility will prove to be a wise investment of time. Too many worthy plans fail because the goal was never realistic in the first place.

Here is one extremely cautious example of testing a goal.

For the project to land men on the moon, the American National Aeronautics and Space Administration (NASA) commissioned three separate independent studies and carried out their own internal study. Afterwards, they had another independent body probe into the four sets of findings. Only after all that evaluation and preplanning was the decision made to go ahead[33].

That was extremely cautious but in proportion to the boldness of such a vast new undertaking.

At the other end of the spectrum, every day thousands of leaders commit to new goals without pausing to assess feasibility. Perhaps they assume their vast experience makes that step unnecessary. Or perhaps they subscribe to the idea that positive thinking is all powerful and will overcome every obstacle. Whatever their thinking, or lack of thinking, many later realize that a little structured feasibility study upfront would have revealed they were attempting the impossible.

At this point, some readers may be feeling a powerful urge to skip forward and move past checking feasibility and to get stuck in to making progress.

Other readers will feel more accepting of the idea that it pays to pause and check feasibility. That difference is an example of how much our personality can influence our default style of leadership.

So, if you feel drawn to jump past feasibility, it would be wise to pause and think, 'I should reflect upon what I should do rather than what I want to do.'

33. Sources: *Chariots for Apollo: A History of Manned Lunar Spacecraft* by C. Brooks, J. Grimwood and L. Swenson (1979) NASA Archive: *Apollo spacecraft feasibility study*, Wikipedia

Consider this. In 2002, a study into information technology projects concluded that 87% of them failed to achieve the original goals, either wholly or in part. The most frequent reason for failure was that the goal was not totally feasible in the first place.

A nationwide survey in New Zealand in 2010 indicated that two thirds of organisations experienced at least one project failure during the previous year; only one third of projects had been delivered on budget, leading to a loss of approximately NZ$15 million. So much wasted...

On rare occasions, we accept a low threshold for certainty: *'We don't know if it possible, but we think it is a good idea and we are going to try.'* However, for the vast majority of our goals, before we start, we need to know that not only are we going to succeed but also within an acceptable time.

How certain do you need to be at this stage? Your answer will depend upon several factors:

- Will this be a first, or has it been done before?
- Will you be carrying out more of the same work you know inside out, or will you be performing new tasks in which your team has little experience?
- Do you have access to all the necessary knowledge and experience?
- What would be the consequences of failure: insignificant, middling or massive?

When you study feasibility you usually discover challenges you would have later stumbled into unprepared. That enables you to look for solutions, change your approach or even modify your goal. Your pre-planning may convert a lost cause into a potential winner. There is another massive benefit from studying feasibility.

When the team starts work on this goal, you will want to convince everyone to believe in forthcoming success, and you can only do that if you personally truly believe it can be done. Your belief will empower your actions and inject enthusiasm into team members.

Considering your current goal, the following is a checklist that should help evaluate feasibility.

Feasibility Checklist

1. Is the goal defined beyond doubt, so that everyone can understand what is going to be achieved and everyone can agree when it has been achieved?
2. What significant objectives must be achieved along the way?
3. What skills will you need? Does your team possess those skills? If not, can you access them from elsewhere?
4. What resources will you need? Do you have access to them when you need them: Machinery and equipment? Training? Knowledge? Materials? Finance? What else?
5. What work must be done sequentially, thereby possibly extending the time required for completion?
6. How long will it take? Do you have that time available? Is there a time limit and can it be done within the time limit?
7. What will it cost? Is that cost acceptable? Is there a maximum cost limit?
8. What work can be done in parallel, thus potentially saving time?
9. What collaboration will you need from outside your team? Will that be available when you need it?
10. What can you predict might go wrong? Are those risks acceptable?
11. How will you monitor progress so that you know you are on the way to success?
12. What else needs to be considered?

The answers to the above twelve questions enable you to ask yourself, *'Am I confident enough to proceed?'* If the answer was YES, you are ready to progress. If the answer was MAYBE or NO, then the situation is not positive, but you may still be able to rescue the goal. Maybe you can canvass more expert opinion. There may be someone within your team who has useful experience or knowledge or you could enlist external expert professional help. And finally, could the goal be modified in some way to make it attainable and still satisfy everyone concerned?

If, after all those considerations, you remain convinced the goal is impossible there will be little point in committing to try and achieve the impossible. If you have a boss, it could be that he or she should become more involved at this stage. Which raises the question of bosses...

If you need to gain approval from others before you can alter course, then your written feasibility study will provide the ammunition to support your case. If you do not enjoy the type of working relationship with your boss where you can easily discuss changing course, read the suggestions for managing upwards in Chapter 16.

CREATE YOUR VISION

Having read all that information about goals setting, you may wonder why this mode is not called *Goal Setting* instead of *Vision*. The difference is important.

A goal definition is a dry, factual, definitive statement, while a vision is an emotive depiction. For example, we referred to President Kennedy and his goal to send men to the moon. He did not merely announce:, *'We will send men to set foot on the moon and bring them back within eight years from today.'* Kennedy went further and gave us a masterclass in how to share a vision.

Re-read Kennedy's speech on page 51 and you will find his words create pictures in your mind. His descriptive language triggers within us a visual, auditory, and kinaesthetic response. Kennedy's words engage our senses. For example, we can easily imagine the roar of that giant rocket taking off. His listeners in that football stadium could look at the length of the football field in front of them and imagine the awe-inspiring size of the rocket. Some of the people in his audience may have felt internal warmth as Kennedy described the intense heat of re-entering the earth's atmosphere.

You want to generate the extra motivation that comes when your team feels emotionally involved. Emotions literally grab a bigger slice of brain activity and in so doing generate thought and action[34]. And that is why leaders who create a vision succeed more often than those who simply define goals.

As you write your vision, use words that convey an accurate and vivid description. Include words that enable people to taste, see, feel, smell, and hear what it will be like to achieve some of the key objectives necessary and the end goal itself. Do not exaggerate, but do paint a vivid picture that people can see in their mind's eye. Write your vision as a very short speech. If you restrict yourself to under three hundred words you will be able to deliver your text in under two minutes. That text will prove useful, not only as a reference that you may later want to copy and paste into other documents but also to repeat when you induct new recruits to your project.

SUMMARY

Your objectives when leading in vision mode are:
- Have a clearly defined goal because you can only achieve a goal when you know exactly what it is.
- You believe it is feasible within an acceptable degree of certainty that you and your team can achieve the goal in the timescale required, to the agreed standard and

---

34. To read more about the rapidly developing area of neurology, you may enjoy *The Neuroscience of Emotions* by Professor David D. Franks, Virginia Commonwealth University, available online.

with the resources you have available (labour, skills, materials, time available, outside support, etc.)

- You have created a vision of the goal which will help you to enthuse and motivate others.

Achieve those three objectives and you create a platform for lift-off. One can only say, *'Well done'* – your work in Vision Mode is done for now.

In the usual sequence of events your next mode of action will be Plan Mode, but just in case, reassess your perceptions as per Chapter 9 and your team members' perceptions as per Chapter 10.

'The very essence of leadership is that you have to have a vision. It has got to be a vision you articulate clearly and forcefully on every occasion. You can't blow an uncertain trumpet.'

Theodore Martin Hesburgh, 1917–2015
President of the University of Notre Dame for 35 years

CHAPTER 12

LEADERSHIP MODE PLAN

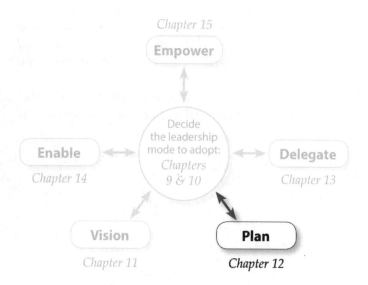

Objectives in Plan Mode
- You have a workable plan for how to achieve your goal that has...
  ... passed critical scrutiny.
  ... been agreed with the person or people who set the goal/s.
  ... where necessary, been agreed with all who have a stake in the achievement of the goal.
- You truly believe you and your team can achieve the goal in the timescale required, to the agreed standard and with the resources you have available: people, skills, materials, time, support, etc.

ABOUT PLANNING

How much time would you usually devote to planning before getting on with the job?
- People with an aptitude for detail, procedures and processes tend to enjoy planning.
- People who are naturally risk-averse are in danger of too much planning and too little action.
- People with an inbuilt sense of urgency and a strong drive to achieve frequently become frustrated by the planning process and so avoid planning. They sometimes produce quick results and dramatic success but also risk dramatic failure. They often make mistakes that a little more forethought would have prevented.

As you know from previous chapters, as a leader it is important that we understand ourselves so that we can modify our actions to do what we should, rather than what we prefer. That applies to every aspect of leadership. As Cicero[35] so

---

35. Marcus Tullius Cicero, 106–43BC, Roman lawyer, politician, orator and Consul of the Roman Republic.

nicely put it, *'It is absurd that a man should rule others who cannot rule himself.'*

There is another attitude that can prevent adequate planning — the belief that plans are not worth the effort. The man in charge of invading France from England on D-Day (June 6, 1944) was General Dwight D Eisenhower, who later became President of the United States. He said that *'Plans are worthless, but planning is everything.'*

Eisenhower was commenting on the fact that few plans work out as hoped. There are usually unforeseeable events along the way that create difficulties that undermine our original plans. But, as Eisenhower continued, 'Planning is everything.' He referred to the fact that working from a plan makes it so much easier to adapt to new circumstances and get back on track. Or put another way, the *cliché* holds true — failing to plan is planning to fail.

Without adequate planning, even the simplest goal takes longer and results in a lower quality outcome at a higher cost, just as the trainees in Chapter Two discovered when they redecorated the two offices. The group that engaged in planning started work two hours later but completed the job quicker.

The other important benefit of planning is that having a credible plan enables you personally to truly believe that you will succeed. Your plan verifies that you can do the work in the time required, to the necessary standard and with the available people, skills, materials, etc.

Your personal belief plays a crucial role in making you sound more convincing when you tell everyone that *'We can do this and we will do it well.'* And when your team sees how you operate from a well-thought-out plan, they will be persuaded of forthcoming success. Thus, your plan plays an essential role in motivation as well as organisation. But how much time should you devote to planning?

Many experts recommend that leaders devote around fifteen percent of time to planning to leave 85% available for action[36].

---

36. Example: *Managing Agile Projects* by Sanjiv Augustine (Prentice Hall,2005)

That is a bit inflexible. How about you devote the minimum time you find necessary to feel confident that you can complete all the steps in your plan and get them right without having to redo work? This is a reasonable test to help you avoid missing any essential steps or carrying out the work in the wrong sequence. You need a plan that will avoid nasty surprises that you could easily avoid with a little more forethought.

Whilst you are reasoning that out, you may even discover some insurmountable barrier to achieving your goal. In which case, at least you identified the problem early enough to have a fighting chance of finding a solution. If you cannot, knowing early will reduce the seriousness of the consequences.

TEAM MEMBERS PERCEIVING THAT *'I AM NOT CONFIDENT IT IS POSSIBLE.'*

When team members are not confident that their objectives are possible, we know that lack of belief will handicap their performance. When several team members feel negative about the challenge ahead, their lack of confidence spreads to infect your entire team, which saps energy and destroys performance. There are two probable causes for this.

1. Team members do not currently understand how it can be done, which displays a need for more careful delegation.
2. The team is correct, it cannot be done. That means you must consider your options, the first of which is to switch back to Vision Mode and think through how to react to this news. Remember, leadership is rarely a well-ordered linear progression.

Some leaders are tempted to convince others through force of personality, skilled rhetoric and a display of personal belief. This is the *'It can be done because I say it can be done'* approach to leadership. It may work, but only for as long as the leader is proved to be correct.

Inevitably, the leader will eventually claim something to be possible and they will be wrong. From that moment on, the team will ignore the leader's enthusiastic proclamations as mere hype. His or her leadership credentials have been undermined, possibly forever. Thus, hype is only a short-term crutch.

The best solution is always for each team member to understand exactly how to achieve their individual objectives. Nothing beats a workable and realistic plan, executed by people who, through the competence of their leader, believe in the outcome.

CREATE THE PLAN

You should by now have determined your goal to be feasible. If not, consider the feasibility checklist in Vision Mode, Chapter 11. Your feasibility study will have already started the planning ball rolling. The next step is to develop that into a complete plan.

Planning a project has become synonymous with complex computerised planning software, and the need for training to understand all the jargon, charts and systems involved. Professional planners take exams to gain qualifications and certification for joining a professional body[37]. That elevated level of knowledge is advantageous if you tackle mighty and complex projects.

However, your projects may not require such a sophisticated approach.[38] Before resorting to outside help and computerised planning systems, consider what level of detail you need to account for these common requirements:

1. What are the many objectives you must achieve along the way to attaining your end goal?

---

37. For example, the Association for Project Management, Project Management Institute.
38. Computerised project planning and management systems fall outside the scope of this book. Suggested reading for learning more about these systems: *Computer-Aided Project Management* by George Suhanic Oxford University Press,2000)

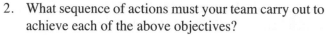

2. What sequence of actions must your team carry out to achieve each of the above objectives?
3. Which are the types of activity that your people can work on concurrently, to facilitate progress?
4. How long will each piece of work take to complete?
5. When must each piece of work be completed, and thereby when can each following dependent piece of work commence?
6. What are the major milestones at the end of each major section of work that will help you check progress is satisfactory?
7. Who will do the work and can you have the necessary people available as and when required?
8. Will any training be necessary to fill gaps in the skills required?
9. What materials, equipment and supplies will be required?
10. What contributions will you require from outside your team: actions, support, supplies, etc.?
11. How will you monitor progress against your plan, to enable you to adjust it if necessary?
12. How will you measure successful achievement in terms of time taken, cost, quality, etc.?

Having considered the above list, here are two telling additional questions:

o Are you experienced in creating plans that answer the above questions and produce a plan from which you, and others, can work?
o Do you have a track record for completing the execution of similar plans and achieving the end goals on time and satisfactorily?

If the answer to both the above questions is 'YES' you are obviously expert at creating realistic plans in your field of work and implementing them. If you do not feel so confident, then you will almost certainly benefit from reading the 'how to plan' guides in Chapters 17 and 18.

Whatever planning method you use, there is one recommended last step which has transformed many questionable plans into reliable blueprints for success. Professional planners will choose to have their work checked by an independent expert, or experts, who have not been involved so far. That separation is essential because people who work on a plan can easily become blind to its deficiencies.

Do not fall into the trap of assuming your plans are flawless. Instead, presuppose you have at least one hidden glitch in there somewhere, lurking, ready to trip you up at some later date. Expose the inevitable faults. We are too close to our own plans, too invested in their success. We can even become blind to problems that others would find glaringly obvious. Protect yourself by choosing at least one suitably experienced person to review your plan. Tell them you expect them to spot the 'holes' in your work. Missing out this step will almost certainly prove embarrassing and expensive.

Planning Mode Checklist
- Your goal is defined in writing.
- Your goal is agreed with the 'sponsors' of the goal: boss, client, etc.
- You have created a plan that is sufficiently detailed to enable the well-organised execution of the plan and attainment of the goal.
- Your plan has been approved by an independent expert or experts as viable and workable.

When your plan is complete you are ready to move on to the next appropriate mode of leadership. In the usual sequence of events, this will be Delegate Mode, where you convert your plans into action and results.

Most importantly, you need to believe in your plan wholeheartedly, because your belief will empower you to act confidently, which will in turn inspire others.

You may need to return to Plan Mode if events conspire to drag you off-course, and you need to adjust your plan in response. As you get closer to achieving your goal, your re-planning time will reduce.

After planning, you will often immediately start to delegate the work, which is discussed in the next chapter. However, whenever you feel that you have completed your work in any mode of leadership, it is wise to pause and reflect upon your own and team members' perceptions about the work ahead. To do this, consider the perceptions diagrams on pages 138 and 139 before you move forward into your next mode of leadership.

Eventually, through familiarity, this process will feel natural as you repeatedly learn, think, decide and then take action.

'Good fortune is what happens when opportunity meets with planning.'

Thomas Alva Edison, 1847-1931
American inventor of the phonograph, the motion
picture camera, the long-lasting light bulb,
sound recording and more.

CHAPTER 13

LEADERSHIP MODE: DELEGATE

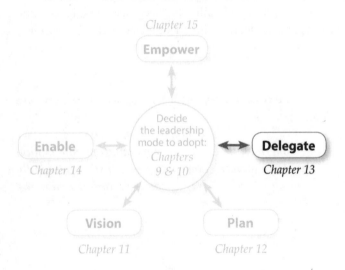

- Every current item of work has been delegated effectively.
- Each team member understands their individual objectives, which includes what they must do, how to do it, when it must be done and to what quality or measurable outcomes.

ACTIONS IN DELEGATE MODE

In Vision and Planning modes you concentrate upon doing the right things. In Delegate mode, you focus on doing those things right, which requires coordinating who does what and when.

You act in delegate mode when:

A. You have completed your work in Plan Mode, you have established success criteria, and it is time to start working to achieve your goal, OR

B. Your perceptions match those stated opposite, OR

C. Team members' perceptions match those opposite.

You divide up the work and delegate the objectives and tasks. You want people to be thinking something like this, '*I know exactly what I am supposed to achieve and how to do my work*'. And if the work is going to be challenging and difficult you also want them to think that '*I may find this a demanding task that will stretch me, but I know I can do it.*'

When someone genuinely holds those confident opinions, you could say that employee is 'switched on.' Short of something unforeseen going wrong, he or she is likely to perform well and achieve the objective.

Often, managers will interpret an employee's negative response as their fault and indicative of a bad attitude or laziness. In fact, the fault is more often caused by ineffective delegation.

If people respond negatively when you delegate work to them it is important to discover the reason for their response. Have they understood correctly? Did they perceive the work as too difficult? Do they see problems ahead that you need to be aware of? We want to make it possible for employees to succeed. And we want them to feel positive about the work ahead. If they do not, it pays to find out why and take appropriate corrective action.

As leader of a large organisation, you will be able to delegate managing the detail to other senior people. You delegate major objectives and leave the senior manager to divide up the work and handle the detail. But still read what follows because your own delegation process sets the standard that others will follow.

In delegate mode, the leader converts the plan into action by dividing work so that each individual task is coordinated with all the others. You break down your plan into manageable chunks of work that can be handed to individuals or groups of people.

You may already have a favourite method for dividing up the work. If that has proven successful, then great. If not, you may benefit from the method of creating a work breakdown structure like the one described in Chapter 18. Once you have divided the work into suitable portions, you can set about delegating the work.

Having divided the work into delegable chunks the leader needs to delegate effectively, not merely dish out the work with minimal oversight and assume all will pan out fine. That would be abdicating responsibility and a route to disappointment.

DELEGATION GUIDELINES

1. Where you have a reliable manager reporting to you, delegate a block of suitable work for him or her to divide up and supervise. Check back with the manager occasionally to monitor progress.

2. Consider the available people resources. If all the work you delegate adds up to more than the time available during any day or week, you need to amend your plan or recruit extra help.

3. You do not need to know exactly how every tiny piece of work will be done, but you do need to be sure that the people who do the work have the necessary knowledge. Are there any gaps between the knowledge of your people and the knowledge required to complete the work? If so, you will need to find a way to plug those gaps with training, by importing extra people or exporting some of the work.

4. When giving work to very capable people, delegate the objective and let them utilise their ability by deciding the fine detail of how to set about achieving the objectives.

5. Put it in writing. Describe what you want achieved. Define a successful outcome so that completion can be checked against that definition, agreed beyond doubt, and celebrated. Set a target time for completion or an absolute deadline when essential. Include all necessary detail to avoid misunderstandings.

6. Always get people to agree that timelines and deadlines are realistic and achievable. It is no good forcing people to agree to deadlines they do not really think they can meet. You need people to truly believe it is possible. If they do not, dig to find out why, and work on creating solutions. Handle those difficulties up front and you reap the reward later.

7. Do not always give the worst jobs to the best people. This can have your highest performing people bogged down in problems when they could otherwise be making much more significant progress for you.

8. If people are less capable, it will be necessary to delegate the sequence of smaller tasks that add up to achieving the objective. That requires closer oversight and micro-management. You want to avoid that whenever possible

because it can quickly absorb a large portion of your valuable time.

9. Make sure all the necessary materials and resources are going to be available when required such as tools, equipment, money, etc.

10. Having delegated effectively, leave people to get on with their work, but maintain control. Diarise for yourself exactly when you will check on progress against the plan. Keep that appointment with yourself. It is just as important as delegating the work in the first place.

HOW TO JUDGE YOUR SUCCESS IN DELEGATE MODE

When you have delegated chunks of work effectively you will see that...

... each person understands their individual objectives.

... each team member knows exactly what they must achieve and how to do it.

... everyone understands by when they must complete their tasks.

... each objective has a defined and measurable outcome that you will be able to tick off a list when completed.

Delegating the maximum number of low-level tasks to others frees your own time. You can devote more time to focussing on the high-level leadership activities as you learn, think, decide and act.

AND FINALLY

You will need to return to Delegate Mode periodically until you have attained the end goal. To decide which mode of leadership to adopt next, consider your situation by again reviewing the Leader's and Team Members' Perceptions.

'No man will make a great leader who wants to do it all himself, or to get all the credit for doing it'.

Andrew Carnegie, 1835–1919,
who rose from poverty to be the richest man in the world
(peak wealth $309 billion dollars at 2017 value)
and then gave away 90% of his fortune.

CHAPTER 14

LEADERSHIP MODE: ENABLE

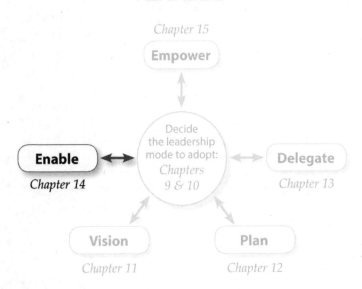

> **Objectives in Enable Mode**
> * Everyone knows what to do and how to do it.
> * We have all the necessary skills at our disposal.
> * No inadequacies or deficiencies disrupt progress.
> * People are working together effectively.
> * Our progress is on time and up to the standard required.
> * I am confident we are progressing towards achieving all our current goals and objectives. Team members also display confidence.

In a perfect world, we would delegate objectives and then move on to other matters. Soon, people would report back with, *'Job done, what do you want next?'*

The leader's life is rarely that easy, but we can make it easier by acting in Enable Mode. You do this...

... after you have delegated a volume of work to team members, or

... when your perceptions match those stated opposite, or

... if team member's perceptions match those opposite.

Your time spent acting in this mode will probably increase as you approach the attainment of your goals.

LEADER'S ACTIONS IN ENABLE MODE

1) Walk the floor

Walking the floor is an old management tactic where a manager would leave his or her office and walk around a factory or shop floor to see for themselves what was really happening. In fact, older readers may recall that some managers had the job title of 'Floor-Walker.'

No matter what type of organisation you work in spending time amongst the front-line workers is highly recommended. You learn so much about the realities of the work in hand

and you cement your position as part of the team. You can spot things that may not be going to plan. You get to check that supervisors and more junior leaders feed back to you all relevant information. You spot opportunities for efficiencies and improved coordination. Of course, workers will ask you when they want some assistance to make their lives easier, or the work more efficient.

2) Learn, think, decide, and act

Ask people how they are getting along with their work. Avoid questions that will merely elicit a yes or no response. Ask open questions such as *'How's it going?' 'Tell me about that.' 'What do you think?' 'How can we do this better?' 'What challenges do you see ahead?' What's going well and what's going not so well?' 'What could we do to make the work easier / faster / better?'* That invites people to 'open-up' and reveal their true opinions. They may deliver unpalatable news. But if you are leading effectively they may also mention how well the team works together.

Be attentive and listen carefully. You will surely learn much about your people, their work and how to accelerate progress. You want to promote an atmosphere of openness that reveals all relevant truths. Whenever blame and criticism rises to the surface you re-frame that into positive action with a response such as, *'That is interesting. So, what do you think might be the solution?'* You set a positive tone by your example of always focussing on solutions and progress.

And then you act. You always act. To continuously learn, think, decide, and act are vital leadership traits.

3) Lead from the front

In Enable Mode, you are amongst the action, so now is an appropriate time to roll up your sleeves (metaphorically or actually) and prove that you are not afraid of hard work. People will more easily follow a leader who shows the way through his or her own actions.

4) Catch people doing things well

Find people doing things right. That gives you the opportunity to say, *'Excellent work. Well done.'* Praise, justly earned, is always welcome and people respond with renewed enthusiasm. And other people who observe you delivering praise will redouble their efforts in the hope of you also recognizing their efforts.

5) Be steadfast when appropriate

At this stage of a project, obstacles tend to arise and undermine team confidence and test your own steadfastness. If that happens, reflect upon the care you have taken during Vision and Plan Modes to ensure your goal is feasible and attainable. Having become confident that it can be done in the Vision and Plan Modes, at this later stage uncertainty is an insidious enemy. It steals in and saps team resolve, belief and performance. At the first signs, quash such thoughts within yourself. Let your team see how you remain focused upon getting the work done and overcoming any hurdles.

6) Achieve the leader's objectives in Enable Mode

1. Check that everyone knows what to do and how to do it.
2. Make sure that you have all the necessary skills within the team, or available from outside.
3. Look for any inadequacies or deficiencies that may disrupt progress, and resolve them.
4. Look to make sure that your people are working together effectively as a team, supporting each other and not merely focussing on their individual attainment.
5. Check that progress is on time and up to the standard required.

When you have completed the above tasks and you feel confident you are progressing towards achieving all the current objectives, you are ready to change leadership mode. Again, check the leader's and team members' perceptions (pages 138 & 139) and select your next mode of action.

'Whatever course you decide upon, there is always someone to tell you that you are wrong. There are always difficulties arising which tempt you to believe that your critics are right. To map out a course of action and follow it to an end requires courage.'

Ralph Waldo Emerson, 1803-1882,
Philosopher and essayist, writer of 'Self-Reliance.'

CHAPTER 15

LEADERSHIP MODE: EMPOWER

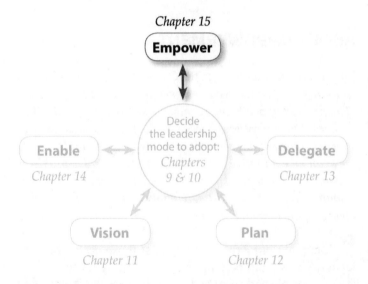

Objectives in Empower Mode

- Our progress is on time and I am confident we are moving toward success with little or no reliance upon my input.
- Much of my time is free to invest in planning for the future.

You act in Empower Mode when…

… People know what should be achieved and how to do the work.

… People have the necessary skills and resources.

… No inadequacies or deficiencies hold the work back.

… Everyone works together effectively.

ABOUT EMPOWERMENT

Empowerment, according to the Oxford English Dictionary, is *'Authority or power given to someone to do something'*, and *'The process of becoming stronger and more confident.'* The Business Dictionary adds a more work-related description: *'… sharing information, rewards and power with employees so they can take initiative and make decisions to solve problems and improve service and performance…giving employees skills, resources, authority, opportunity, motivation, as well as holding them responsible and accountable for the outcomes of their actions.'*

Compare your experience against those definitions. As leader, you should be empowered to lead your team. You are responsible and accountable for their results. You should be trusted to produce results without close supervision from above. As a result, you will feel motivated to do your best work without someone having to watch over you and tell you to get on with it.

Thus, you know what being empowered feels like. You should be experiencing the highs that come from…

... meeting challenges and overcoming them yourself.
... realising your personal potential.
... learning and growing through your work.
... receiving respect for your achievements.
... knowing you achieve goals through your personal talents and effort.
... feeling the drive to achieve and the willpower to follow through with actions that lead to results.

Those factors create emotional highs. When you empower team members you make it possible for them to experience higher levels of satisfaction, even to self-actualise[39]. And the rewards for you are three-fold:

1. People are likely to operate at peak effectiveness, or close to it.
2. You supervise less and achieve more
3. You release time to invest in high value activities such as planning for the future.

To empower people, you give them operational freedom. You delegate the objective and let them get on with the work to produce your desired outcome without you closely supervising them. If they ask for support, you remain available, but you relinquish much of the burden of control.

If you are the boss of a large organisation, you should frequently be able to act in Empower Mode because you should have a senior team of very capable people. You delegate the objectives and leave your senior people to achieve them.

If you run a small team, most of whom report directly to you, then you will need to consider each person, one by one, and the objectives they currently work upon.

If you have been an effective leader when acting in Vision, Plan, Delegate and Enable modes, and if you have capable people

---

39. Self-actualization: 'The realization or fulfilment of one's talents and potentialities, especially considered as a drive or need present in everyone.' Oxford English Dictionary

in your team, it should be possible to empower some people and step back from managing them in detail.

Be sensitive to the fact that some people will never want to accept full personal responsibility and will fall apart if you give them freedoms and responsibilities that others would relish. Those people will always need close supervision. Do not think less of them for they will also have their value. Curiously, we find it is often the person with rare and irreplaceable skills who falls into this category.

And be aware that some projects will never allow you to operate in Empower Mode. This could be because they involve rapidly changing circumstances which demand frequent re-planning. Or perhaps the work pushes your team to the boundaries of their skills and so you must maintain a watchful eye over performance.

LEADER'S ACTIONS IN EMPOWER MODE

Look for people to empower. These will be team members who know what to do and how to do it. No inadequacies hold them back and you feel confident their progress will not be negatively affected by other people or outside influences. You feel confident that you can leave them to get on with the work. They can achieve their individual objectives on time and to a satisfactory standard.

Having delegated the objective and left someone to do the work, back off, but observe how they cope. Demonstrate trust with words such as, *'I'm confident you can do this.'* Provide an emergency safety blanket with something like, *'If necessary, if you have doubts, call on me.'* You do not abdicate responsibility because you monitor progress. You agree a time in the future when you will review progress. Make that an appointment and keep it. Most often, people rise to the occasion. And by giving them the opportunity to prove themselves you help them grow and develop.

Some types of work demand close supervision from start to finish. In those situations, you may never get the opportunity to operate in Empower Mode. However, if you feel that in your line of work you must always manage the detailed work, hold on a moment. Right now, question your motives. Are you in danger of becoming a little bit too much of a control freak, as they say? Or could it be that you have not devoted enough attention to training up your people? And have you set up administration systems that remove the necessity for people to habitually refer to you?

Not loosening the reins a little can hold others back and severely curtail your own achievements. Effective leadership demands letting other people rise to the occasion and do the work instead of you. To help you decide if you are missing opportunities to empower others, reassess the appropriate mode of leadership for individuals or the entire team by consulting the perceptions diagrams on pages 138 and 139.

Henry Ford loved to empower others to work with little supervision while he retired to his office to think. He used to say that *'Thinking is the hardest work there is which is the probable reason so few engage in it.'* Very true. Being able to empower others is the pinnacle of leadership because it sets you free to really concentrate upon learning and planning future progress.

'A leader is best when people barely know he exists, when his work is done, his aim fulfilled, they will say, "We did it ourselves."'

Lao Tzu, 6th– 5th Centuries BC,
Chinese philosopher, founder of Taoism.

PART FOUR

'HOW TO' GUIDES

Refer to the following guides when necessary, or when suggested in the previous chapters.

'Leadership and learning are indispensable to each other.'
John F. Kennedy 1917–1963,
35th President of the United States

CHAPTER 16

MANAGING UPWARDS

For you to be a successful leader you need to enjoy a healthy, positive relationship with your boss or bosses. That will make your work life more agreeable, increase your job satisfaction, aid your career and enable you to tackle tricky situations such as telling the boss that he or she cannot have what they want.

Bosses vary. A few are brilliant, inspiring and helpful. They make our job easier and we find it a pleasure to work with them. Other bosses are insecure or indecisive and avoid decision making, which can make life more difficult. Some bosses jump to conclusions without properly considering the consequences of their decisions. Some think they know it all and will not accept anyone else's opinion. Some communicate so poorly that you can never be certain about what they want.

Some bosses are so hands-off that you receive no support and must act in a vacuum. Many more will want to micromanage everything, which undermines your authority and slows down progress. Worse still, it encourages your team to circumvent you and go direct to the 'real' boss. And if you report to multiple bosses your life becomes more complicated.

That paints a bleak but realistic picture. Sadly, the overall quality of leadership is poor. The American pollster Gallup surveyed one million workers and learned the main reason they quit their jobs was because of an unsatisfactory boss or immediate supervisor.[40] What a waste.

Unless you are unusually fortunate, to ensure a productive relationship with your boss, you will need to manage upwards. This is not currying favour but making your working relationship more effective. Here are some suggestions to help you do that.

- Your boss is like a very important client. You sell your services to him or her, and in return you receive an income. Therefore, treat your boss like a very important customer. Deliver a quality service and do your best not let him or her down.

- Know your boss. Do this by putting yourself in your boss's shoes. What does he or she personally need, want and care about? As the American Indian proverb goes, *'To understand a person we must walk a mile in their moccasins.'*

- Just as team members tend to live up or down to your expectations, so do bosses. Display an expectation that your boss will manage you effectively, and with a little luck he or she will try harder not to let you down.

- Proactively communicate. Remove the boss's doubts about what is happening by taking the initiative to regularly inform him or her.

- Find out how your boss prefers to receive information. Is it phone, email, face to face, by appointment, a casual meeting in the corridor, a short or lengthy report, chatting after work, coming into work early and using the quiet time before the day starts, meeting in the bar, or whatever. Adopt his or her preferred method of communication even if it is not your personal favourite.

- We relate best to people like ourselves. You can appear more like your boss with a little effort. When you speak with your boss, match his or her preferred style of

---

40. Source: Gallup, Inc., www.gallup.com.

speech, be it fast or slow, quick paced or thoughtful, hard or soft, blunt or considerate of other's feelings. You want your boss to think, *'I can relate to this person.'*[41]

- We might not manage to make it so our boss likes us, but we can make our boss respect us, which may be even better. For example, always deliver on your promises. If that is not going to be possible, tell the boss about the coming problem sooner rather than later. Always speak of solutions, never blame. Never unjustly claim the credit for successes, but do let the boss know about your major accomplishments. Never shirk responsibility and shift blame when things go wrong. Always demonstrate an admirable work ethic. Support your boss though thick and thin (provided he or she is not doing something illegal, unethical or stupid). That describes the sort of person you want working for you and that your boss does too.

- Be positive. Never, ever gripe at work. If you must let off steam, do it outside of work where there is no chance that your comments will ever be repeated back at work. That way, your boss will never see you as part of the problem, but instead as part of the solution.

That list sets a high standard for your behaviour but is it not the person we all aspire to be?

A final thought. Having a boss is a little like being in a marriage where you do not get to choose your partner. It is probably by far the best solution for all concerned if you can make the relationship work. If you 'divorce' your boss and move to a new position, with so many low-quality bosses out there, your next boss may be even worse.

---

41. Consider learning more sophisticated communication skills involving gestures as well as language and speech patterns. For example, read *How to Speak So People Really Listen: The Straight-Talking Guide to Communicating with Influence and Impact*, by Paul McGee, (Capstone, 2016).

Through your intelligent actions you may be able to engineer a working relationship with your boss that allows you to do an excellent job and realise your potential. However, if after trying all the above remedies you go home feeling unhappy, knowing that in your situation you can never prosper, it is probably time for more drastic action.

'A man should look for what is, and not for what he thinks should be.'

Albert Einstein, 1879-1955
German-born theoretical physicist,
most famous for his theory of relativity.

CHAPTER 17

PAPER BASED PLANNING

You need a large flat surface such as a desktop, a whiteboard, or an office wall. Next, you want a pad of those sticky yellow paper pads such as PostIt[42] notes. You proceed as follows:

1. Brainstorm
2. Sequence and divide into work streams
3. Add milestones
4. Calculate how long the plan will take to execute and establish the critical path
5. Take steps to avoid becoming a victim of the Planning and Team Scaling Fallacies
6. Add a contingency to your plan
7. Check your belief

BRAINSTORM

You brainstorm everything you can think of that needs to be done: individual objectives, the end goal, whatever comes to mind. It is important, especially when brainstorming with

---

42. PostIt® is a registered trademark of the 3M Company.

others, to follow a few simple rules that protect and enhance creativity.

BRAINSTORMING RULES

Step One:
Accept all ideas as valid and record them quickly, without pausing to critique. At this stage, do not question any ideas, no matter how silly they might at first appear. Negative thoughts kill creativity so only positive thoughts may be expressed. Encourage everyone to contribute because often the quiet people come up with ideas that others would forget. No interruptions allowed until afterwards because they will kill the flow of ideas.

Step Two:
Take a break. When the mind relaxes after an intense brainstorm, more valuable ideas will pop into the mind. Write them down immediately or you will forget them again. Seems crazy, but that is how it works.

Step Three:
After your break, collect any extra ideas onto sticky notes. The brainstorm is now complete and you may switch into critique mode.

After the brainstorm, you take each paper note and improve the wording of each objective so it accurately describes what must be achieved. Remember, each objective is just one of the many that will be necessary to attain the end goal. Some pieces of paper will describe necessary tasks. Some ideas and notes, after careful reflection, will not be worth keeping. You discard those as irrelevant and add any more ideas that come to mind.

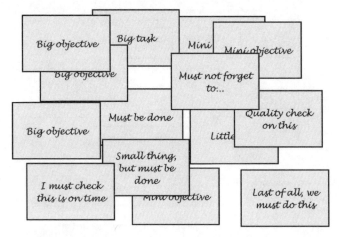

Brainstorm tasks, objectives, and everything relevant to achieving the goal

SEQUENCE AND DIVIDE INTO WORK STREAMS

Commencing some tasks will require the prior completion of others, so you start to move tasks and objectives into sequence. Place first tasks on the left and position others with time progressing to the right.

As you re-order the tasks and objectives, you will find the work naturally splits into several streams of activity that you can have people working on concurrently. For example, the planning exercise for redecorating the office[43] easily fell into four streams of activity: 1) Monitor progress and (if necessary) adjust plan, 2) Source the paint and other materials, 3) Prepare the room and surfaces for painting, 4) Apply the paint. Different people could simultaneously work on these four streams of activity.

---

43. Chapter two, page 34

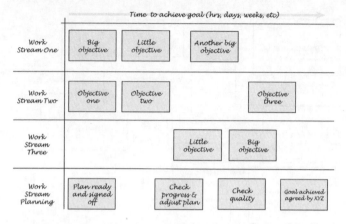

	Time to achieve goal (hrs, days, weeks, etc)				
Work Stream One	Big objective	Little objective	Another big objective		
Work Stream Two	Objective one	Objective two		Objective three	
Work Stream Three			Little objective	Big objective	
Work Stream Planning	Plan ready and signed off		Check progress & adjust plan	Check quality	Goal achieved agreed by XYZ

Organise the work into time-sequence and divide into work streams

As you review all your PostIt notes, you move individual tasks and goals to show the sequence of work progressing horizontally from left to right. You are creating a timeline as your plan begins to take shape.

ADD MILESTONES

Around this point, you will find there are some important milestones along the way. For example, these could be significant points that mark the completion of one type of work, a significant achievement, or a sensible juncture at which to review progress. You create PostIt notes for each milestone and add them to your plan. You might use different coloured paper to make these stand out. Milestones are events and therefore of zero duration. All the time, you continue to improve your plan as you arrange the pieces of paper into their correct sequence of events and horizontal position along your developing timeline.

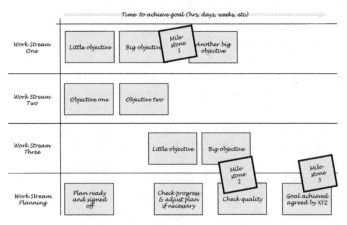

Add milestones and improve sequence of events

CALCULATE HOW LONG THE PLAN WILL TAKE TO EXECUTE AND ESTABLISH THE CRITICAL PATH

There is a popular formula used by many project managers to estimate the time required to complete a task. The biggest advantage of using a formula is probably that it encourages people to think more carefully about how long it will take to do something.

It is worth quickly trying this technique for yourself. Think of an important task that your team will soon undertake.

   a.   What is the best, carefully considered, estimate of how long it will take? Multiply the answer by four and note the result. Note that time.
   b.   Now be optimistic. If everything went very well, what is the shortest time required to complete the task?
   c.   Now be pessimistic. If things go badly, how long could it take? Note that time.
   d.   Finally add the three above results and divide by six, which gives you a weighted average for estimated time required

As a formula, it looks like this:

Best estimate: T_m

Optimistic estimate: T_o

Pessimistic estimate: T_p

$(4T_m + T_o + T_p) \div 6 =$ Weighted Average Estimate[44]

Try that method for a while and you will probably discover, as others have, that averaged across many tasks and objectives it helps you produce more reliable time estimates.

Once you estimate how long it will take to complete each piece of work you can horizontally total all the items. Now you can vertically total how many hours of work this adds up to for each day or week. That will enable you to check that you have sufficient people available.

There will be one special string of tasks, each of which cannot be started or finished until prior tasks have been completed. This will be the string of tasks which will take the longest time to complete. This will show the shortest time in which your goal can be achieved. If just one of that string of tasks were to be delayed it would slow down your entire project.

That series of key events is called the critical path (see diagram opposite). You need to be aware of and manage the critical path carefully or each small delay will potentially add a significant amount of time to achieving your end goal.

It is possible to establish the critical path for less complex projects without resorting to a computerised planning system. Doing that will greatly improve your ability to achieve your goals on time, on budget and to the quality desired.

If the plan becomes very complex because there are too many variables involved for you to easily establish and calculate the critical path, it may be advisable to switch to a software based planning tool such as Microsoft Project, Jira, Slack, Wrike and others. However, there is now a wide variety of competing systems, many of them cloud based. You may

---

44. This is the Three Points Estimate method, as frequently used with PERT (program evaluation and review technique).

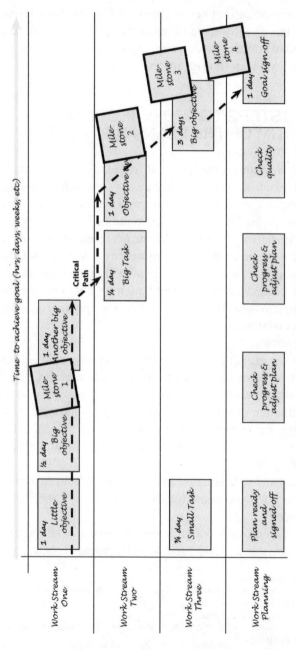

Add time taken, improve sequence and calculate critical path

Time to achieve goal (hrs; days; weeks; etc)

Work Stream One

1 day
Little objective

½ day
Big objective

Mile-stone 1

1 day
Another big objective

Critical Path

Work Stream Two

¼ day
Big Task

1 day
Objective 2

Mile-stone 2

3 days
Big objective

Mile-stone 3

1 day
Goal sign-off

Mile-stone 4

Work Stream Three

¾ day
Small Task

Work Stream Planning

Plan ready and signed off

Check progress & adjust plan

Check progress & adjust plan

Check quality

find one especially suited to your type of work. Search online for 'planning software' and 'project management software.'

And next there is another important issue to consider. How accurate are your time estimates?

TAKE STEPS TO AVOID BECOMING A VICTIM OF THE PLANNING FALLACY

People are outrageously optimistic when they estimate time[45]. We all do it to some extent. We humans seem to have an inbuilt optimism which surfaces in various ways, one of them being that we are inclined to underestimate how long things will take, typically by between forty and fifty percent. In 1979, this theory was named the Planning Fallacy[46]. Various academic studies have refined our understanding. For example, in 1994, a class of students were asked how long it would take them to complete their theses. On average, they predicted 34 days. The actual time taken averaged 56 days, forty percent longer than estimated.[47]

We see examples around us every day as people regularly complete work later than promised. On a grander scale, governments spend large sums to employ experts who plan infrastructure projects such as new roads, buildings, offices, railways, airports etc, which often take twice as long and cost double the estimate, or worse. Those underestimates are often caused by the Planning Fallacy and the Team Scaling Fallacy.

You can, to a large extent, protect yourself from the Planning Fallacy when you allow for its effects. Here is some useful guidance:

- Our estimates of time become more accurate when we are asked to name and consider potential obstacles that

---

45. Law Eight in *The Secret Laws of Management*, by the author, Headline Publishing (2010).
46. Daniel Kahneman and Amos Tversky.
47. Study published by Buehler, Griffin & Ross, Journal of Personality and Social Psychology (1994).

we may have to overcome.[48] This means you would be well advised, as part of your planning process, to have people list potential obstacles and problems that could slow progress.

- The further ahead we predict the more likely we are to underestimate the time required to do things.[49] This effect is thought to be a consequence of far off obstacles apppearing less significant to us than those we may soon face. Thus, if you ask someone to predict how long a task would take to complete starting tomorrow their estimate will be less optimistic than if you ask them to plan to start the task several months ahead. This means you should probably approach every planning exercise as if you start tomorrow.

TAKE STEPS TO AVOID BECOMING A VICTIM OF THE TEAM SCALING FALLACY

If two people can do a job in four days, how long will it take four people to complete the same work? Half the time, two days? That seems logical but it would depend upon many factors, such as how much of the work can be carried out concurrently and will it help or hinder to have more people working in the space available. However, people consistently have unrealistic expectations of how much it will help when you add more people to a team.

This effect is called the 'Team Scaling Fallacy' and can be very significant when you plan work involving more people than you usually assign to a task[50] To help protect yourself against this fallacy, subdivide the plan into small chunks of

48. Peetz, Buehler, & Wilson, Journal of Experimental Social Psychology (2010).
49. *Prediction: The Inside View* by David Dunning in Social psychology: Handbook of basic principles (Guilford Press, 2007)
50. *The team scaling fallacy: Underestimating the declining efficiency of larger teams* by B.R. Staats, K.L Milkman and C.R Fox (Organisational Behavior and Human Decision Processes, 2012).

work, down to a scale you are familiar with. That may mean it takes you longer to create your plan, but it will go a long way towards protecting you from the effects of the Team Scaling Fallacy.

ADD A CONTINGENCY TO YOUR PLAN

No matter how hard we try, something generally happens that we could not plan for, which hinders progress or increases costs. So, don't forget to add a little extra time and budget to allow for the unforeseen.

How much extra time or money you should add on is difficult to predict. This may help you decide. If you have never done something similar before, even after your best planning efforts you might be 50% inaccurate regarding total time and cost. But if you have considerable experience in tackling the work, you may be capable of planning time and cost within 5% accuracy.

CHECK YOUR BELIEF

The greatest advantage of having a realistic plan is probably psychological. Niggling doubts dissipate. The leader's belief intensifies, and that conviction spreads amongst the team.

'To accomplish great things, we must not only act, but also dream, not only plan, but also believe.'
François-Anatole Thibault, 1844–1924,
French novelist, journalist and poet.
Winner of the 1921 Nobel Prize for Literature.

CHAPTER 18

DIVIDING THE PLAN INTO DELEGABLE PORTIONS

Too much preparation and organisation can create a bureaucratic burden that hinders progress, so it is very tempting to skip straight to the action and start as soon as possible. However, at some point you need to break down the work into delegable portions that enable you to tell people what they must do and coordinate their work with others. This chapter provides a little more detail in how to go about that.

This is time-consuming, detailed work you may choose to delegate to someone with appropriate experience and later check the result. The important thing is that you have the delegation tools you need.

1) Break down the work

You already have a plan that includes a series of steps and sequence of objectives. Completing all those steps will lead to achieving the end goal. If you used the paper planning method described in the previous chapter, your plan will look something like the diagram on page 129 which is repeated overleaf with an illustration of breaking down two items from the plan into further detail.

For each task and objective, you subdivide the work into actions. You divide the detailed plan into pieces that are small enough to...

...   delegate as one piece of work.
...   enable someone to check each piece of work is completed.

As you do this, you may discover previously overlooked steps in the plan. If so, adjust the plan accordingly.

Many items in your plan will rely upon the previous completion of one or more steps. Check you have those chunks of work in the correct sequence.

Usually, the planner will want to break down all the work ahead into detailed chunks before starting to execute the plan. This reduces the likelihood of missing any essential chunks of work. However, sometimes you need to have already completed some work before you can be sure of all the subsequent actions required. In this case, you will need to break down work for the current phase of your plan and then keep ahead of the game as the plan progresses[51].

2) Create delegation documents

A written delegation document is not the sole means of delegating but an important supporting record. It provides a definite statement to refer to and evidences what must be done[52]. This avoids misunderstandings, which are a frequent cause for people not getting it right first time. And it forces a disciplined approach to delegating work which prevents many management errors.

The document includes the following information, as necessary:

• What must be achieved? Define the task/work/outcome/ objective.

---

51. Often referred to as 'rolling wave planning.'
52. You may benefit from checking the delegation guidelines from Chapter 13.

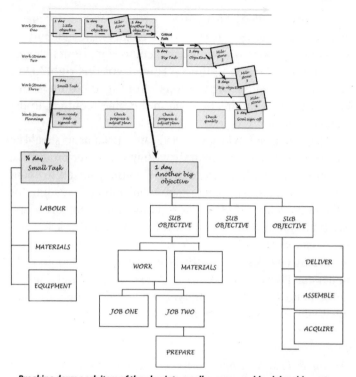

Breaking down each item of the plan into smaller, manageable, delegable parts

- Why is this necessary? How this work meshes with other work.
- Who will do it? Name the person delegated to, who will assist, who will support, who will manage.
- How will we know when the work has been completed satisfactorily? Describe the standards required: quality/cost/etc.
- Where will the work be done? Include location when relevant.
- When must it be done? Start and finish dates/times, maximum or minimum time allowed.
- What resources will be available and/or required? For example: time, people, materials, equipment, external / supplier's contributions, etc.

In some situations, both parties sign the delegation document. People who casually accept work verbally will suddenly sit up and take notice when you ask them to sign. Both manager and employee pause to think, 'Have I got this right? Do I fully understand the implications? Am I ready to make this commitment? Can this be done in the time required, to the standard required?'

The format and style of your delegation documents should be succinct and to the point. Wordy writing is counter-productive because people will not read it all. Confine yourself to about 200 words maximum. That is about one minute's reading for an average adult.[53] Let people read the document and allow them an opportunity to digest the content and ask for any necessary clarification.

When you delegate work, it is crucial that people fully understand what you want. Do not just accept a brief, hurried agreement. Insist on certainty, even having people explain what you are asking them to do, just to make sure.

'If you don't know where you're going, you will probably end up somewhere else.'

Laurence J. Peter, 1919–1990,
Canadian educator and management theorist,
best known for the Peter Principle.

---

53. One minute delegating is an idea proposed in *The One Minute Manager* by Kenneth Blanchard and Spencer Johnson (William Morrow & Co, 1982) .

PART FIVE

QUICK REFERENCE

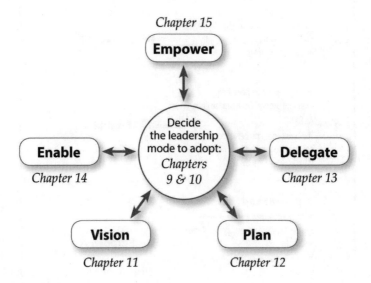

Chapter 15

Empower

Enable

Chapter 14

Decide
the leadership
mode to adopt:
*Chapters
9 & 10*

Delegate

Chapter 13

Vision

Chapter 11

Plan

Chapter 12

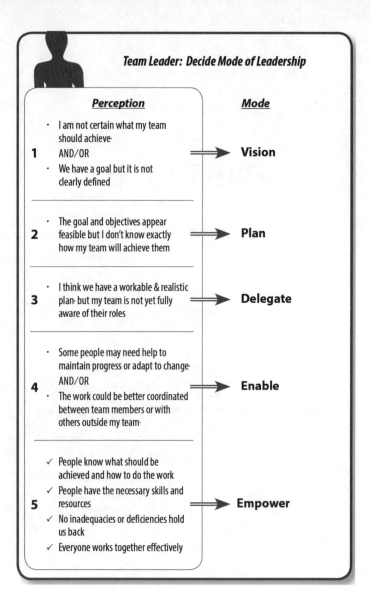

Team Leader: Decide Mode of Leadership

Perception		Mode

1
- I am not certain what my team should achieve
- AND/OR
- We have a goal but it is not clearly defined

➡ **Vision**

2
- The goal and objectives appear feasible but I don't know exactly how my team will achieve them

➡ **Plan**

3
- I think we have a workable & realistic plan but my team is not yet fully aware of their roles

➡ **Delegate**

4
- Some people may need help to maintain progress or adapt to change
- AND/OR
- The work could be better coordinated between team members or with others outside my team

➡ **Enable**

5
- ✓ People know what should be achieved and how to do the work
- ✓ People have the necessary skills and resources
- ✓ No inadequacies or deficiencies hold us back
- ✓ Everyone works together effectively

➡ **Empower**

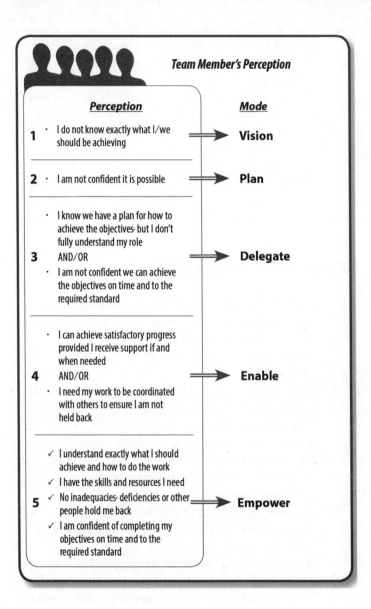

Team Member's Perception

	Perception	_Mode_
1	• I do not know exactly what I/we should be achieving	**Vision**
2	• I am not confident it is possible	**Plan**
3	• I know we have a plan for how to achieve the objectives, but I don't fully understand my role AND/OR • I am not confident we can achieve the objectives on time and to the required standard	**Delegate**
4	• I can achieve satisfactory progress provided I receive support if and when needed AND/OR • I need my work to be coordinated with others to ensure I am not held back	**Enable**
5	✓ I understand exactly what I should achieve and how to do the work ✓ I have the skills and resources I need ✓ No inadequacies, deficiencies or other people hold me back ✓ I am confident of completing my objectives on time and to the required standard	**Empower**

> **Objectives in Vision Mode:**
> - You have a clearly defined goal because you can only achieve a goal when you know exactly what it is.
> - You believe it is feasible within an acceptable degree of certainty that you and your team can achieve the goal in the timescale required, to the agreed standard and with the resources you have available (labour, skills, materials, time available, outside support, etc.)
> - You have created a vision of the goal which will help you to enthuse and motivate others.

FEASIBILITY CHECKLIST

1. Is the goal defined beyond doubt, so that everyone can understand what is going to be achieved and everyone can agree when it has been achieved?
2. What significant objectives must be achieved along the way?
3. What skills will you need? Does your team possess those skills? If not, can you access them from elsewhere?
4. What resources will you need? Do you have access to them when you need them: Machinery and equipment? Training? Knowledge? Materials? Finance? What else?
5. What work must be done sequentially, thereby possibly extending the time required for completion?
6. How long will it take? Do you have that time available? Is there a time limit and can it be done within the time limit?
7. What will it cost? Is that cost acceptable? Is there a maximum cost limit?
8. What work can be done in parallel, thus potentially saving time?
9. What collaboration will you need from outside your team? Will that be available when you need it?

10. What can you predict might go wrong? Are those risks acceptable?
11. How will you monitor progress so that you know you are on the way to success?
12. What else needs to be considered?

DELEGATION GUIDELINES

1. Where you have a reliable manager reporting to you, delegate a block of suitable work for him or her to divide up and supervise. Check back with the manager occasionally to monitor progress.

2. Consider the available people resources. If all the work you delegate adds up to more than the time available during any day or week, you need to amend your plan or recruit extra help.

3. You do not need to know exactly how every tiny piece of necessary work will be done, but you do need to be sure that the people who do the work have the necessary knowledge. Are there any gaps between the knowledge of your people and the knowledge required to complete the work? If so, you will need to find a way to plug those gaps, with training, by importing extra people or exporting some of the work.

4. When giving work to very capable people, delegate the objective and let them prove their ability by deciding the fine detail of how to set about achieving the objectives.

5. Put it in writing. Describe what you want achieved. Define a successful outcome so that completion can be checked against that definition, agreed beyond doubt, and celebrated. Set a target time for completion or an absolute deadline when essential. Include all necessary detail to avoid misunderstandings.

6. Always get people to agree that timelines and deadlines are realistic and achievable. It is no good forcing people to agree to deadlines they do not really think they can meet. You need people to truly believe it is possible. If they do not, dig to find out why, and work on creating solutions. Handle those difficulties up front and you reap the reward later.

7. Do not always give the worst jobs to the best people. This can have your highest performing people bogged down in problems when they could otherwise be making much more significant progress for you.

8. If people are less capable, it will be necessary to delegate the sequence of smaller tasks that add up to achieving the objective. That requires closer oversight, micro-management. You want to avoid that whenever possible because it can quickly absorb a large portion of your valuable time.

9. Make sure all the necessary materials and resources are going to be available when required such as tools, equipment, money, etc.

10. Having delegated effectively, leave people to get on with their work, but maintain control. Diarise for yourself exactly when you will check on progress against the plan. Keep that appointment with yourself. It is just as important as delegating the work in the first place.

PLANNING SEQUENCE

1. Brainstorm
2. Sequence and divide into work streams
3. Add milestones
4. Calculate how long the plan will take to execute and establish the critical path
5. Take steps to avoid becoming a victim of the Planning and Team Scaling Fallacies
6. Add a contingency to your plan
7. Check your belief

Brainstorming Rules

Step One

- Accept all ideas as valid and record them quickly, without pausing to critique. At this stage, do not question any ideas, no matter how silly they might at first appear. Negative thoughts kill creativity so only positive thoughts may be expressed.
- Encourage everyone to contribute because often the quiet people come up with ideas that others would forget.
- No interruptions allowed until afterwards because any interruption will kill the flow of ideas.

Step Two

- Take a break. When you relax after an intense brainstorm, more valuable ideas will pop into the mind. Write them down immediately or you will probably forget them again. Seems crazy, but that is how it works.

Step Three

- After your break, collect any extra ideas onto sticky notes.
- The brainstorm is now complete and you may switch into critique mode.

Objectives in Enable Mode

- Everyone knows what to do and how to do it.
- We have all the necessary skills at our disposal.
- No inadequacies or deficiencies disrupt progress.
- People are working together effectively.
- Our progress is on time and up to the standard required.
- I am confident we are progressing towards achieving all our current goals and objectives. Team members also display confidence.

LEADER'S ACTIONS IN ENABLE MODE

1. Walk the floor
2. Learn, think, decide and act
3. Lead from the front
4. Catch people doing things well
5. Be steadfast when appropriate
6. Achieve the leader's objectives in Enable Mode

Objectives in Empower Mode

- Our progress is on time and I am confident we are moving toward success with little or no reliance upon my input.
- Much of my time is free to invest in planning for the future.

LEADER'S ACTIONS IN EMPOWER MODE

Look for people to empower. They will be people who...

   ... understand exactly what they should achieve and how to do their work.

   ... have the skills and resources necessary.

   ... are not going to be held back by inadequacies, deficiencies, or problems caused by other people.

   ... will feel confident they can complete their objectives on time and to the required standard.

   ... you feel confident about.

AFTERWORD

Dear Reader,

Some final thoughts for you...

Firstly, I expect that at some time whilst reading this book you have noticed I do not promise instant solutions or an easy ride but quite the reverse, because effective leadership requires continuous thought and deed. But then, nothing much of value was ever gained without effort. Success generally comes at a price: continuous, persistent endeavour. But that should not put you off, because the more we practise the easier it gets. Do not allow yourself to shirk the effort and fail to rise to the leadership challenge.

Next, about learning. You have probably come across the quotation, allegedly from the Chinese teacher Confucius, '*I hear and I forget. I see and I remember. I do and I understand.*' Teaching was mostly verbal in ancient times but is often written today, so I want to amend the quote to '*I read and I forget. I see and I remember. I do and I understand.*' That applies to the content of this book. You may well forget some of what you have read. However, Confucius was correct in that sight and pictures form the bedrock of our memory[54] so I recommend you review the illustrations herein. And most crucially...

---

54. There is much research proving this to be the case. For example, the recent Harvard study by Dr. Kosslyn and Carol Seger [citation?]

When we look back over our lives so far, gathering knowledge is only helpful if we put it into practice. Nothing beats 'doing' to help us remember, understand, and benefit. I urge you to use the five modes of leadership. Pause to consider each situation you are faced with as you manage people and lead your team. Use this book to help you decide the most appropriate mode of leadership for the occasion. Next, decide what actions to take and then get on with it. The sequence is to repeatedly learn, think, decide, and act.

Appropriate positive action is the key to experiencing increased control over events and people. As a result, people will more willingly follow you and help you achieve your goals.

Thank you for reading this book. I wish you every success.

Stuart Wyatt

'Your actions become your habits,
Your habits become your values,
Your values become your destiny.'
Mohandas Karamchand Gandhi, 1869—1948,
Indian activist who led the nation of India against British
rule, often called the father of India.

ABOUT THE AUTHOR

Stuart Wyatt is a businessman with over forty years of experience as a manager and leader.

Stuart's first management role was at age twenty-six, when he became national sales and marketing manager for the outboard motor division of Volvo-Penta UK. He switched to the expanding information technology sector during 1979. He founded, expanded and sold his own company, Wyatt Computer Supplies. He was Managing Director of Multisoft Solutions, a systems house serving manufacturing and retail.

In the late 80s, Stuart developed and published the SERAfile® personal productivity system. For ten years, Wyatt & Associates provided productivity training and leadership mentoring for managers at all levels to client SMEs and large enterprises including many household names.

In the 1990s Stuart returned to 'doing' rather than teaching. He has provided interim executive support to companies in the UK and US, including managing the launch of new ventures, marketing campaigns, interim general management and business strategy projects.

Stuart says that, "Managers and leaders at all levels are short of reading time. Therefore, I aim to give them a concise and interesting read. I focus on practical, real-world solutions that leaders can start using immediately combined with a reference guide to enhance their leadership for many years to come."

Stuart is married and lives in the West of England.

--

www.stuartwyatt.com

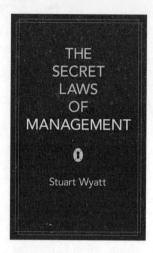

THE SECRET LAWS
OF MANAGEMENT

40 Essential Truths
for Managers

by Stuart Wyatt

ISBN-13: 978-0755360949

"The Secret Laws of Management distils the 40 sacred truths about business for supervisor and subordinate, trainee and old hand."

LiveMint.com & The Wall Street Journal

"Stuart's book has really been a great primer on what exceptional management is all about. I really wish I'd had this tool years ago. It might have saved many a frustrated employee!"

Alex Fielding, CTO, Power Assure, Inc.

"This is the way all business books should be written, with compelling ideas organized in a real-world way. As you face the daily challenges of managing or leading you can return to this book for inspiration and practical ideas for almost any leadership challenge. We acquired a company this year and this book should be required reading for anyone who is planning on acquisition or merger. The section on change is particularly relevant to the bringing together of two companies."

Justin Hersh, CEO, Group Delphi

"This book has muscle and sinew that have been exercised in real life competition. Tightly written, no holds barred. Every executive could use it as a tune up checklist. A standout piece of work."

Anthony Sandberg, President, OCSC Sailing